More praise for Let Us Keep The

Summer and winter, day and night, wor⌐
with these rhythms of life. This booklet introduces us to the rhythms of
Christian life as lived according to the seasons of the Church year, with
its feasts and fasts, its high-days and holidays. Helpful, challenging, and
instructive: I recommend it.

> **Dr. Michael Ward**
> *Author of* Planet Narnia: The Seven Heavens in the Imagination
> of C.S. Lewis
> (original endorsement for the *Holy Week & Easter* edition)

This book is very good. It is well-written, geared to the non-specialist
reader who hasn't got a lot of time on his/her hands, and very practical.
It ought to do very well and only hope that the other books in the series
live up to this one.

> **Gerald Bray**
> *Research Professor of Divinity, Beeson Divinity School*
> *Author of* God is Love *and* The Doctrine of God
> (original endorsement for the *Epiphany & Lent* edition)

This is an utterly delightful book! It's filled with wisdom and warmth.
Here you can learn about diverse ways Christians prepare for and cele-
brate the birth of Christ. I've been studying, writing about, and practicing
these traditions for years, yet I learned many new things in these pages.
This is the perfect book for parents who want to deepen their children's
experience of Advent and Christmas. Lots of truth here, as well as practi-
cal, fun ways to celebrate the birth of Christ.
If parents were to ask me how to enrich their families' celebrations of
Christmas, *Let Us Keep the Feast* would be my top recommendation.
Solidly biblical, faithful, and fun, Let Us Keep The Feast is the perfect
book for families who want to enrich their celebrations of Advent and
Christmas.

> **Rev. Dr. Mark D. Roberts**
> *Foundations for Laity Renewal, Kerrville, TX*
> *Author,* Discovering Advent: How to Experience the Power of
> Waiting on God at Christmastime
> (original endorsement for the *Advent & Christmas* edition)

I really loved this book because it brings together the liturgy of the
church and the life of the family.

> **Timothy George**
> *Founding dean of Beeson Divinity School of Samford University*
> *Chairman of the Board for the Chuck Colson Center for Christian*
> *Worldview*

Let Us Keep The Feast is a wonderful introduction to the gift of the Church Seasons. Not only is the spiritual purpose of each Season clealy articulated, but creative and practical suggestions will surely help individuals and families grow in Christ. I can't wait to see the rest of the Seasons presented!

The Rev. Karl E. Dietze
Rector of Trinity Anglican Church in Bakersfield, CA
(original endorsement for the *Advent & Christmas* edition)

Brilliant and illuminating: that is the what I have found living the Church Year to be and what this book is.

John Mark N. Reynolds
Provost, Houston Baptist University
(original endorsement for the *Holy Week & Easter* edition)

Let Us Keep The Feast is a rich, yet practical, guide for the celebration of the Church Year in the home. Replete with explanations of each season, the biblical basis for its celebration, and ideas for its observance, this book will be a valuable source for individuals and families seeking to infuse their Christian walk with the treasures of Church year observance. I look forward to Advent and Christmas as my family and I will be using these practical suggestions for celebrating the season.

The Rt. Rev. Dr. Eric Vawter Menees
Vth Bishop of San Joaquin
(original endorsement for the *Advent & Christmas* edition)

Protestant retrieving the Church calendar is one of the most important and encouraging signs of renewal that I know. This short introduction to two important seasons is everything an introduction should be: theologically astute, clear, practical, and properly introductory. It knows just how much people new to these practices might need to get started with a big list of resources for those who want more. I highly recommend it.

Matthew Anderson
Author of The End of Our Exploring and Earthen Vessels
(original endorsement for the *Epiphany & Lent* edition)

Christianity takes time seriously, and there is something special and holy about celebrating the church year in the home as a family. I'm delighted to see this volume on Epiphany and Lent, and I believe it provides a wonderful resource to individuals and families who want to take seriously the sacred rhythms of a life in Christ. *Let Us Keep the Feast* is a bountiful blessing!

Peter Barnes
Senior Pastor, First Presbyterian Church of Winston-Salem, NC
(original endorsement for the *Epiphany & Lent* edition)

As I read this book, I felt so much peace and joy in thinking about the many ways we can orient our lives to Christ's story. In my busy, urban, context, I long for meaningful, embodied ways to connect with Jesus. Let Us Keep the Feast will be a great blessing to me and the fast-moving city dwellers I minister to.

Julie Barrios
Director of Spiritual Formation at Reality SF
(original endorsement for the *Epiphany & Lent* edition)

Jessica Snell has put together a simply invaluable resource for all of us, engaging doctrine, imagination, and the desire to engage deeply with the truths of Christian faith. Whatever our level of familiarity with Christian tradition, there is so much here to refresh and renew us not just for one year but for many to come. We are indebted to her and to all who have contributed to her fine work.

Ann Loades CBE
Professor Emerita of Divinity, University of Durham and Honorary
Professor of Divinity, University of St Andrews
(original endorsement for the *Holy Week & Easter* edition)

Many people are rediscovering the hidden treasure of the church seasons, and especially the slow savouring of our salvation story throughout the Church Year. *Let Us Keep The Feast* provides an excellent resource for those who would like to make this journey together.

Malcolm Guite
Author of Sounding the Seasons, Seventy Sonnets for the
Christian Year
(original endorsement for the *Holy Week & Easter* edition)

The authors usher us into complementary seasons of the Christian Year in ways designed for home and heart. And these welcome and winsome encouragements come spiced with fresh resources for us and our families: scriptures, songs, poems, prayers, recipes and creative activities that help us dwell in the story of Christ artfully. Indeed, let us keep the feast with this spread of delectable servings.

Bobby Gross
Director of Graduate & Faculty Ministries for InterVarsity
Christian Fellowship
Author of Living the Christian Year
(original endorsement for the *Epiphany & Lent* edition)

The nurturing potential of what these writers suggest is truly tremendous. To Jessica and the rest of the contributors, heartfelt thanks.

Dr. J.I. Packer
(original endorsement for the *Advent & Christmas* edition)

Accessible for the newcomer to liturgical tradition and informative even for those raised with it, *Let Us Keep The Feast* is packed with guidance as well as ideas for crafts, music, art, and poetry for adults and children. I look forward to using its recommendations.

> *Karen Lee-Thorp*
> *Author of* Story of Stories: A Guided Tour from Genesis to Revelation
> (original endorsement for the *Holy Week & Easter* edition)

Its simplicity will give comfort and clarity to readers who have not yet celebrated the Christian calendar, and its sincerity will rally readers who have followed it their whole lives. It is practical and generous, stuffed with craft ideas, recipes, references to Auden or Eliot's poems, and heartfelt reflections–a delightful, edifying mixture.

> *Peter David Gross*
> *Executive Director of Wheatstone Ministries*
> *Editor of* The Examined Life
> (original endorsement for the *Epiphany & Lent* edition)

I am pleased to commend to you this wonderful little book on the Church Year entitled *Let Us Keep the Feast*. It will be helpful to anyone who wants to better understand and experience the spiritual growth that comes from living out the Christian Calendar. Each chapter ends with a number of suggestions to enrich the season, and this provides a variety of resources appropriate for children and families at home — music, fun activities, poetry, prayers, Scripture verses, and other suggested readings. I highly recommend it for any parent who wants to enhance the Sunday morning experience at Church by supplementing it with what takes place at home during the week.

> *The Rt. Rev. Jack Leo Iker*
> Bishop of Fort Worth
> (original endorsement for the *Holy Week & Easter* edition)

Søren Kierkegaard, the "Melancholy Dane," dourly observed, "The reason why people celebrate on New Year's Eve is to drown out the sound of grass growing over their own graves." Christians have a more hopeful reason for marking time, a reason rooted in the incarnation, crucifixion, resurrection, and ascension of Jesus, and the promise of consummation. This helpful series encourages us to explore in accessible, imaginative, and informed ways the distinctive hopefulness of the Christian vision of time through everyday practices and reflection.

> *Allan Poole*
> Pastor of Blacknail Presbyterian Church of Durham, NC
> (original endorsement for the *Epiphany & Lent* edition)

In a day of nonstop multisensory overload, these writers beckon us into the contemplative and sacred space of the church's calendar and focus our senses on the festive delights of Christian reflection and worship. For those of us who feel adrift in a culture spinning and swirling without orientation, *Let Us Keep the Feast* can recalibrate our lives, centering our hearts on Christ and anchoring our practices in church and home within the lively traditions of the saints.

Andrew Byers
Chaplain of St Mary's College, Durham University
Author of *TheoMedia: The Media of God in the Digital Age* and
Faith Without Illusions: Following Jesus as a Cynic-Saint
(original endorsement for the *Epiphany & Lent* edition)

Let Us Keep the Feast: Living the Church Year at Home is indeed a feast, and one at which Christians from all traditions may dine and be filled. Written with clarity and creativity, it is a delightful introduction to the seasons and practices of the Christian year, and a sure guide to living them out in a family setting.

Rev. Dr. Joel Scandrett
Assistant Professor of Historical Theology
Director of the Robert E. Webber Center, Trinity School for Ministry
(original endorsement for the *Epiphany & Lent* edition)

Ever since Robert Webber introduced American Evangelicals to Ancient-Future worship in his books and workshops, there has been a need to provide also user-friendly explanations and resources to compliment the public aspects of corporate worship with accessible tools to grow the individual [and the Christian family at home] in their personal spiritual growth. Traditional books of piety are often incomprehensible to people new to the ancient traditions of the Church, besides often being meager in Scriptural references and overwhelming in non-Biblical legends and traditions. These authors do a brilliant job of explaining the traditions of the Church Year, firstly from their Scriptural sources, and the earliest primary sources of the Church as it began to create the seasons and rituals that made up the Church Year. The authors also exhibit a wide knowledge of resources in art, music, and literature relevant to the deepening of a Christian's personal encounter with the crucified and risen Lord. Best of all, they provide a variety of activities, recipes, and hands-on-activities which can give a Christian family numerous ways to allow their children to enter into these Biblical events and be transformed as well as informed by them. This series of books on the seasons and celebrations of the Christian year would benefit every Christian household, every pastor's study and every Sunday School resource center.

The Rev Dr Arnold W Klukas
Professor of Liturgy and Spirituality, Nashotah House Theological
Seminary (retired)
(original endorsement for the *Holy Week & Easter* edition)

Let Us Keep The

FEAST

Let Us Keep The

FEAST

Living the Church Year at Home

Edited by Jessica Snell

With contributions from:
Michelle Allen Bychek
Ann E. Dominguez
Anna Moseley Gissing
Cate MacDonald
Lindsay Marshall
Jennifer Snell
Kristen Stewart
Rachel Telander

Let Us Keep The Feast: Living the Church Year at Home

Published by:

Doulos Resources, PO Box 69485, Oro Valley, AZ 85737; PHONE: (901) 201-4612 WEBSITE: www.doulosresources.org.

Please address all questions about rights and reproduction to Doulos Resources:

PHONE: (901) 201-4612; E-MAIL: info@doulosresources.org.

Published 2014

Printed in the United States of America by Ingram/Lightning Source

Cover design by Julie Hollyday, 2013.

This book is printed using archival paper that is produced according to Sustainable Forestry Initiative® (SFI®) Certified Sourcing.

Snell, Jessica, 1980–

Let Us Keep The Feast: Living the Church Year at Home.

ISBNs: 978-1-937063-65-8 (print); 978-1-937063-64-1 (digital)

2014915630

13 14 15 16 17 18 19 20   10 9 8 7 6 5 4 3 2 1

TABLE OF CONTENTS

Introduction

by Jessica Snell

If you want a cup of tea, you boil water in a kettle. The kettle's a wonderful device, and thank God someone invented it. Which of us, wanting a cup of tea, would go to the trouble of inventing a new kind of kettle from scratch?

When it comes to devotional practices, many of us in the Protestant tradition have been discovering that someone already invented the kettle. Our thirst for the presence of God has led us to rediscover the goodness of many old traditions, traditions that may have been passed over or forgotten for a time while our predecessors in the faith dealt with substantial issues of doctrine and dogma.

But church history belongs to all of us, and more than that, *all* of church history belongs to all of us: all 2000 years of it, and not just the last 500. During that history, Christians developed seasonal devotional practices that helped remind God's people of God's mercies.

These practices include some that might be familiar; giving something up for Lent is one of the practices most of us have heard of. Others of us first learn about the church year through the practice of lighting a candle for each of the four Sundays in Advent. Either of these practices is enough to pique the curiosity of an alert believer and to prompt the question: is there more where this came from?

The answer is yes. There is, in fact, enough to fill a whole book. Like this one.

Scripture and Tradition

The church year isn't commanded by Scripture, but it is suffused with

Scripture. The church year is traditional, but those traditions exist because they have been found, over and over again through the centuries, to aid believers in their walks with Christ.

That ritual and rhythm are wise tools for fixing our ever-wandering attention on the goodness of God is clear even as far back as the covenants of the Old Testament. Celebrations like Passover regularly brought the mercies of God to the forefront of His people's minds; the Israelites were commanded to remind themselves of the mighty acts of the Lord, of how He'd saved them, of how He loved them. They were prompted to worship and thanksgiving, to repentance and to joy. We humans forget the Lord's kindnesses so easily, but a yearly cycle of festivals at least makes it *harder* to forget for quite so long.

There is repetition to the practice of celebrating the church year, but the repetition doesn't breed contempt. It breeds comfort. There is a stability in repeating the same seasonal practices from year to year, and yet there is also enough variety in the changing of the seasons that the stability is never dull. We thrive on rhythms like these. We enjoy the change of the seasons each year, but we also enjoy that they are the same seasons every year. I like it when summer cools to autumn, but part of what I like about the change is how familiar that change is.[1]

Just as the changing seasons are familiar to us, the church year will be familiar to some of you reading this book, as it still forms part of the services of denominations such as the Presbyterians, Anglicans, and Lutherans. This book will help you bring the celebration of these familiar seasons from the church sanctuary into your own home. The church year may be more foreign to other readers whose weekly services aren't focused on a liturgical cycle, and yet this shouldn't prevent you from reaping the benefits of the practices outlined in these pages. The observation of the church year isn't meant to fight against the content of Sunday services, but rather to reinforce them in our hearts, minds, and bodies. This book is focused on bringing seasonal Christian traditions into the home, so that our daily routines can be peppered with little reminders of God's goodness and grace. Ideally, we'll all be as aware of God at home as we are at church.

1 See Chapter 25 of C.S. Lewis's *The Screwtape Letters*: "He has balanced the love of change in them by a love of permanence. He has contrived to gratify both tastes together in the very world He has made, by that union of change and permanence which we call Rhythm. He gives them the seasons, each season different yet every year the same, so that spring is always felt as a novelty yet always as the recurrence of an immemorial theme. He gives them in His Church a spiritual year; they change from a fast to a feast, but it is the same feast as before."

And yet there is room to do all of this imperfectly. The traditions of the church year are an aid to devotional life, and not that life itself. The information in this book is meant to enhance your walk with the Lord, and not to supplant it with an anxious hurry to observe the perfect Christmas or holiest Advent. In fact, the best way to approach the church year isn't as a schedule-happy adult at all, but rather, as a small child.

God's Toddlers

I first really noticed the church year when I became a new mother and was looking for ways to explain the gospel story to my young daughter. My devotional life was largely built around reading, but suddenly I was faced with explaining the story of Jesus to a little person who didn't even know her ABCs.

But she could understand pictures and stories. And when I looked around our church I couldn't help but notice as we moved from Advent to Christmas, and from Christmas to Epiphany, that the entire church calendar is set up like the best of preschools. In a year, we were taken through the whole gospel, made to act out the stories, look at the pictures, and sing the songs — even to do our art projects, as we all sat in the pews the Sunday before Easter, folding palm crosses. All of our senses were involved in this annual retelling of the gospel story.

And there's a reason for that. Many of the traditions surrounding the Christian church year developed in periods of history when most of the population was illiterate. The pageantry and pantomime of the church year helped people who couldn't read the Bible remember the stories of Jesus.

Thankfully, the printing press, the Reformation, and many other, smaller societal pressures have brought the Bible into the homes of the faithful. Yet receiving that great good doesn't mean we have to — or should — abandon the traditions practiced by so many faithful Christians before us. We're not children, we're not illiterate, but we're still people with hands, mouths, noses, and ears as well as eyes, and the traditions of the church year are tools that God can use to draw the whole of our constantly wandering attention back to the truth of the gospel. By prompting us to use our whole bodies, the celebration of the church year can draw us into the contemplation of the good news of Jesus with a child-like wonder and awe.

The Church Year and the Gospel

The cycle of the church year follows the structure of the New Testament. The Christian year begins with Advent and the story of the first coming of Christ, which is the same place the synoptic gospels start. Christmas celebrates the incarnation and is followed by Epiphany, the time of the wise men, which celebrates the gospel being revealed to the Gentiles. Then, as we move towards spring, we recount the whole life of Christ, culminating in the crucifixion and resurrection at Easter. The feast of the Ascension follows and then the transition to Pentecost moves us into the story of Acts, which leads to the last season of the year: Ordinary Time, the long second half of the year. Ordinary Time takes up most of the summer and fall and its length reminds us that this is the time that we, the church militant, really inhabit: this time after the coming of the Holy Spirit and before the end of all things. The epistles are a large part of our guide here as we, like the ancient church, put into practice all that we've learned from the gospel story. Then the church year has its close on Christ the King Sunday, when we remember the promise of Jesus' second coming — the story set forth in Revelation. Which brings us back to Advent again.

So, in celebrating the traditions of the church year, we annually retell the gospel story.

Creation and Order

The other thing we do by celebrating the church year is to reconnect ourselves to the creation story. When God made the universe, the temporal order was part of that creation; evening and morning, the sun sets, the sun rises again. We mark the days and the weeks because God made them: a rhythm of work and rest.

God instituted the seven-day week in creation itself, and then remade it when Christ rose on Sunday morning: our weeks now begin with Sunday and the celebration of the resurrection, a constant, over-50-times-a-year reminder of Jesus' triumph over death. So every week begins with hope, and every day's work is done in a universe filled with order and filled also with creative beauty.

Celebrating the church year helps us become more aware of that good order of creation and so can help us to better worship our Creator. A rhythm of morning and evening prayer is a part of most Christian traditions and gives a holy order to the day. Celebrating the resurrection every Sunday gives order to our weeks. And the cycle of the liturgical calendar gives order to our years. All of these regular practices remind us that our whole lives are to be ordered towards the worship and enjoyment of God.

How to Use this Book

It's our hope that this book will help you in your celebration of the Christian church year. This book is designed so that you can begin using it no matter when you receive it. Each chapter covers one season of the church year, starting with Advent and ending with Ordinary Time. You're welcome to begin the book at the beginning and read all the way through, but you can also simply open to the chapter that covers the season of the year you're currently in and start using the information you find there right away. It's also not a bad idea to take a peek at the next season's chapter, in case there are any events you want to prepare for ahead of time.

For ease of use, each chapter follows the same structure, beginning with an *Introduction* which explains the meaning and history of the season, illuminating what it is and why we celebrate it. In other words, the introduction explains which part of the gospel is each season's particular focus.

Next is the *Calendar* section, which explains when the season takes place and which also highlights any special feast days within it.

In the *Traditions* section, you'll learn how each season has been celebrated by Christians throughout the centuries so you can follow in their footsteps. Then, in the *New Traditions* section, we'll suggest even more creative ideas for celebrating the season. These are not meant to replace the traditional practices, but to supplement them. In the *Around the World* section, we highlight Christian traditions unique to their own corner of the globe.

In the Kitchen will provide you with seasonal dishes and *For the Very Young* gives ideas for adapting the traditions of the season so that even the youngest of believers can participate in the celebrations. *Things to Make* details seasonal handicrafts for both children and adults.

Beyond the Home contains ideas for taking your celebrations out to the wider world. All the seasons of the church year celebrate the gospel and so each season provides its own opportunities for charity and evangelism.

Finally, each chapter includes a *Resources* section which contains a list of Scripture readings, other books and readings, music appropriate to the season and, finally, prayers suitable for everything from bedtime devotions to table blessings.

Advent

by Rachel Telander

Introduction to Advent

Advent is one of the hardest seasons of the church year to celebrate in today's culture. As soon as Thanksgiving arrives, we are bombarded by Christmas carols, Christmas decorations, Christmas everything. We are so saturated by Christmas that we often skip over the one of the most important parts: the preparation. You wouldn't throw a party without preparing the food and drinks; you wouldn't visit a friend without getting ready. We are about to remember the most awe-inspiring thing that happened in the whole of history: God becoming man in the glory and mystery of the incarnation. We need to set aside time to prepare ourselves for this — internally and externally.

The word "Advent" comes from the Latin word *adventus*, which means "coming" or "arrival." The season of Advent is the time we remember that period of history when we were still in darkness, waiting for the Light of the World to come. Since the mid-sixth century, the church has set aside the time before Christmas as a time of preparation, fasting, and self-examination. The precise date of its origin is unknown, but there are several Advent homilies by famous figures such as Pope Gregory the Great which date back as far as AD 590.

The Bible is full of passages that reference the themes of Advent. These themes — light coming into darkness, promises being fulfilled, and the redemption of mankind — permeate the pages of Scripture. They are the theme of life, the theme of the Great Story. Some are specific prophecies about the coming Christ, like Isaiah 11's account of the shoot springing from the stump of Jesse. Others are Old Testament stories that foreshadow the events of the New Testament, like the tale of the Israelites' Egyptian captivity. The Israelites' enslavement in Egypt mirrors the situation of the world before Christ's coming. The Israelites were enslaved to the Pharaoh, while the world was enslaved

3

to sin and death. The Israelites were waiting for God's intervention and redemption through Moses, while the world was waiting for God's intervention and redemption through his Son, Jesus Christ.

But perhaps the most famous Advent-themed passage is John 1:1–18. In this passage, all the themes of Advent are described in words which pierce the soul with their profound truth and beauty:

> In the beginning was the Word, and the Word was with God, and the Word was God. He was in the beginning with God. All things were made through him, and without him was not any thing made that was made. In him was life, and the life was the light of men. The light shines in the darkness, and the darkness has not overcome it...The true light, which enlightens everyone, was coming into the world. He was in the world, and the world was made through him, yet the world did not know him. He came to his own, and his own people did not receive him. But to all who did receive him, who believed in his name, he gave the right to become children of God, who were born, not of blood nor of the will of the flesh nor of the will of man, but of God. (1:1–5, 9–13)

This is the true meaning behind Advent. We are preparing ourselves to receive the greatest present the world has ever been given: the Son of God.

Because of Advent's penitential focus, people often notice the similarities between it and Lent. They both are seasons of fasting before major feasts, and in liturgical churches both of them are symbolized with the color purple. However, Advent is not a fast in the same way Lent is. The season of Lent is a deeply penitential fast. Like Lent, Advent is a season of fasting; however, in Advent, the focus is not on personal flaws, but rather on the flaws in all of creation. Advent focuses on the fact that we were under the tyranny of death and sin, and that we needed a Redeemer to save us. The prayers and songs of Advent, unlike those of Lent, are songs of hopeful joy. The words of sorrow are woven with words of promise.

In a way, Christians are *always* in the season of Advent, twenty-four hours a day, seven days a week, 365 days a year. We are in the Second Advent. As we remember Christ's first coming, we are waiting and preparing, in hope and expectation, for His second. Isaiah 11 — which prophesies the first coming of the Christ — can also be interpreted as describing both His second coming and life afterwards: "The wolf shall dwell with the lamb, and the leopard shall lie down with the young goat, and the calf and the lion and the fattened calf together; and a little child shall lead them" (11:6). Despite the joyful thrill of these words, there is an apocalyptic ring to them. Repentance is the final theme of Advent, precisely *because* we are preparing ourselves, even now, for Jesus' arrival in glory and splendor from the right hand of God the Father, and for the day when we will be with Him, in paradise.

Calendar

Advent is relatively simple to figure out on the calendar. The first Sunday of Advent always falls on the Sunday nearest November 30, or St. Andrew's feast day. Alternately, you can find the beginning of the season by simply counting back four Sundays from Christmas Day.

Advent never lasts more than four Sundays and always ends before December 25.

There are two important feasts which take place in Advent: St. Nicholas Day and St. Lucia's Day. St. Nicholas Day is on December 6, which is the anniversary of his death. St. Lucia's Day is on December 13, which was the day of her martyrdom.

Traditions

Advent Wreaths

Advent wreaths are typically wreaths of greenery woven into a circle, with four candles spaced periodically along the sides and a single white candle in the center of the wreath. At first glance, these wreaths may seem to be just another Christmas decoration. However, every detail of the wreath is pregnant with symbolism, telling the story of the season of Advent.

The shape of the wreath itself is a symbol: its never-ending circle reminds us of God and His eternal love for us, His wayward children. It reminds us that darkness will not endure — but God will. The color green represents hope and new life. This is why the greenery that makes up the body of the wreath is traditionally pine, evergreen, or cedar: unlike other trees, these branches never wither and die in the winter. Their constant greenness symbolizes the promise of eternal life. Sometimes, the greenery is decorated with silver and gold tinsel, a sign of the joyful days of feasting to come. Other plants can be added to the wreath to emphasize Advent's themes. Ivy is one of these; it is a climbing vine and it symbolizes humanity holding onto the strength of God. Less frequently, holly and bay are added to the wreath. Holly, with its sharp thorns and crimson berries, reminds us of the crown of thorns that Christ wore on Calvary and the crimson blood that He shed there for us. Bay, also known as laurel, represents the victory over sin and death. In ancient times, winners of competitions wore wreaths of laurels to celebrate their victories.

Traditionally, three of the four Advent candles are purple, while the other is rose. There are four of them because they represent the four weeks of waiting from the beginning of Advent to Christmas Day. Also, the four candles symbolize the four centuries that passed between the prophet Malachi's writings (the last book of the Old Testament) and the incarnation.

The Advent wreath's candles have different meanings according to different traditions. Usually, the first candle symbolizes hope, or expectation, which is the strongest theme of Advent. Throughout the four weeks of this season, we are waiting in hope for the coming of Christ, expecting redemption. The third candle is traditionally named Joy, reminding us of the angels' triumphant announcement to the shepherds. However, the names of the second and fourth candles are not set in stone. Some say that they stand for peace and love, while others say they stand for the shepherds and the magi.

Despite the other candles' changeable names, the first and third candles always stand for hope and joy respectively. The third candle is always a pink or rose color, corresponding with its theme. The change in color reminds us that the third Sunday in Advent is *Gaudete* Sunday, or "Joyful" Sunday. This Sunday is not as focused on waiting for redemption as the other three; rather, it focuses on the joy that comes with the fulfillment of that redemption. In the liturgical Christian tradition, on this Sunday many churches change the vestments and altar cloths from traditional Advent purple to a cheery rose pink.

The last candle on the Advent wreath is the Christ candle, which sits in the center of the wreath, reminding us what we are waiting for through these dark winter days: the coming of Light of the World. It is usually a white or silvery color, and is only lit on Christmas Eve or Christmas Day.

In the home, the Advent wreath typically is lit every night after dinner, accompanied by Scripture readings. Many different schedules of readings can be found online for free, and often churches have their own booklets of Scripture references for Advent. If your church doesn't have its own list of readings, the easiest compilation to find is in *The Book of Common Prayer*, under the Daily Office Lectionary, which has readings for the entire church year in a two-year cycle. If you'd like to compile your own reading list, it would be appropriate to move through the prophecies that foretell the coming of the Messiah, found in the Old Testament books of Amos, Haggai, Isaiah, and Zechariah. Then you can move to New Testament books such as Revelation and Matthew, which contain prophecies of Jesus' return, tying together the relationship between Advent and the second coming.

The Jesse Tree

Though the exact origin of the Jesse Tree is obscure, it's clear that the idea was prompted by Isaiah 11:1: "There shall come forth a shoot from the stump of Jesse, and a branch from his roots shall bear fruit." It has been speculated that this passage, combined with ideas from plays of the genealogy of Jesus from the Middle Ages, eventually gave birth to what we know today as the Jesse Tree.

There are multiple versions of the Jesse Tree today. It can be anything from a poster of a tree with pictures pasted on in lieu of ornaments, to an actual evergreen tree with ornaments signifying stories dangling from its branches. However it's constructed, the Jesse Tree is a creative method of telling the main stories of the Bible through its principal figures, starting with the creation of Adam and Eve and ending with the birth of Jesus. The litany of stories works its way through the genealogy of Christ and tells about the important part each person played in the lead-up to the incarnation. Traditionally, the first story — that of Adam and Eve and the creation of the world — is told on the first Sunday of Advent, and one story is added per day until it is Christmas Day and you have reached the story of birth of Christ.

The traditional main characters of the Jesse Tree are, in order: Adam, Eve, Noah, Abraham, Sarah, Isaac, Rebekah, Jacob, Rachel, Joseph, Moses, Miriam, Deborah, Samuel, Ruth, Jesse, David, Solomon, Hezekiah, Josiah, Isaiah, Elizabeth, John the Baptist, Mary, and finally, Jesus.

Advent calendars

Although Advent calendars are a newer tradition, they are well-known and frequently used, and even secular versions of these calendars can be bought in stores. Advent calendars come in many different varieties, but all of them have the same purpose: counting down the days until Christmas. They usually start on December 1 and end on December

25. Typically, these calendars are simply made of decorated paper and cardboard, with flaps to lift each day as a countdown. Some of the more ornate ones have pop-ups underneath the flaps, and there are even some with small chocolates as a daily Advent treat.

A Simple Season

For those new to celebrating Advent, this may seem like a lot to take in, and perhaps overwhelming. These traditions are meant to enhance the time of preparation, not to take away from the focus of Advent. If making a Jesse Tree and an Advent wreath is too much for busy schedules, then don't get stressed out trying to do both. If practicing many different traditions and activities distracts you from the theme of Advent – preparing for the coming of Christ — then it would be better to choose only one tradition and stick with it than trying to get everything done and get distracted from the true purpose of this season. Remember, the purpose of Advent is to meditate on the coming of Christ, and the wreaths and calendars are meant to point us back to this focus, not to distract us from it.

Fasting
Throughout Advent, remember that this is a season of fasting — not as severe as Lent, but still a fast. Be mindful of diets and little pleasures, and determine what can be sacrificed. (Please see the chapter on Lent for more on fasting.)

Christmas trees
Getting a Christmas tree before Christmas Day does not violate Advent tradition in the slightest. Many people buy one early in December, but leave it undecorated throughout the season of Advent. Undecorated, it acts as a reminder that the joy of Christmas is yet to come; there is no reason for baubles and lights — yet. The tree also points toward the more solemn fast of Lent. It reminds us not only of the coming of the Savior, but of a time when another tree was fashioned into the rough beams of the cross.

New Traditions

As a countdown to Christmas, have children put pieces of hay in a miniature manger — one a day, until Christmas Day. On Christmas Day, place a figurine of baby Jesus in that manger.

A variation of the straw in the manger idea is putting one figure a day in the nativity scene, until Christmas Day. Perhaps place Mary and Joseph at strategic places around the home, slowly moving them closer and closer to the crèche.

Liturgical churches often have special concerts called "Lessons and Carols" during the Advent season. In these concerts, people read passages of Scripture followed by a song which pertains to that passage of Scripture. An example of this is a reading of Luke 1:26–38, the annunciation, and then a performance of an arrangement of "Ave Maria." The combination of classical music and the Scripture readings often sheds new light on old concepts. Consider attending a Lessons and Carols concert in your area.

There are several different variations on Advent calendars. Most of them are simple, child-friendly, and easy to make. One method is to display twenty-five small presents and open one a day until Christmas. Another variation is to bake cookies and frost each one with a number, one through 25. Eat one a day, until Christmas. (Cookies can be frozen to keep them fresh!)

Another way to count down the days until Christmas is to make an Advent chain. These are simple chains made of construction paper, with a Bible verse written on the underside of each chain link. Each day, break a link of the chain and read the verse. *The Book of Common Prayer* has the daily lectionary in the back, which is a great resource for daily Advent verses.

Instead of having the eldest girl as the only participant in St. Lucia's Day celebrations (see the *Around the World* section below), perhaps have all the children partake in making a St. Lucia breakfast. Make something special, have green and red and white table decorations, and use candles.

Around the World

Advent itself is a fairly uniform season in the church and its traditions do not vary greatly throughout the world. However, St. Nicholas Day and St. Lucia's Day, both of which occur in Advent, can add a colorful international flair to your celebration of the season.

St. Nicholas

St. Nicholas was born around AD 275, and was the Bishop of Myra. His feast day is celebrated mostly in the European countries such as Germany, Poland, and Switzerland. It is also celebrated in Russia. Switzerland has St. Nicholas Day parades, including children's parades, torchbearers, dancers, and brass bands. In Germany, the day is celebrated by having a man dressed as St. Nicholas in full bishop's garb visit children's houses and reward them according to their "good deeds," which he has written in a little book.

St. Nicholas is known mostly for his generosity and kind heart; there are multiple stories about his magnanimous deeds. One of the most famous is the story of the three girls. According to the story, St. Nicholas was quite a wealthy man because his father had died and left him a substantial fortune. As he was passing by a house, he heard three young girls crying because their father was indebted to a man and they were to be sold as slaves to pay off their father's debts. After nightfall, St. Nicholas came back to the girls' house, and threw a bag of gold down their chimney to pay off their father's debts. He returned the following two nights, dropping a total of three bags of gold down their chimney, to pay off all the debts and to cover the dowries of the young women.

As you might have guessed, St. Nicholas is the basis for the popular figure of Santa Claus today. However, in reality St. Nicholas was not just a "nice" old saint. He was a major fighter of the Arian heresy in the fourth century and was a key part of the Council of Nicaea. Tradition claims that at one point, he was so sickened by the heresy that Arius (the founder of the Arianism) was speaking that he stood and struck Arius across the mouth.

St. Nicholas Day is on December 6, which is the day the saint died in AD 343. To celebrate his feast day, little children set their shoes outside of their door, with small handsful of hay or carrots in them. These are to feed "St. Nicholas's horse" as he passes by. The legend says that in the morning, St. Nicholas will have filled the children's shoes with small presents, to express his gratitude.

St. Lucia

St. Lucia's Day is on December 13. St. Lucia lived in Sicily, although her feast day is widely known as a Scandinavian holiday. St. Lucia, or St. Lucy, as she is also called, was a saint who lived in the third century.

She is known for her generosity. She would bring baskets and baskets of food to the poor with her mother, and she would wear a wreath of candles on her head to light the way. She is also known for her purity and devotion to Christ. She had vowed to remain a virgin all her life. The man to whom she was betrothed was furious when she refused to marry him, and had her killed. She is honored as a martyr in the Roman Catholic Church.

St. Lucia's Day is widely celebrated in Scandinavia. On the morning of December 13, the eldest girl of the household gets up before the rest of the family, dresses in a white dress which is usually tied with a red sash — to remember St. Lucia's purity and martyrdom — and, like St. Lucia, wears a crown of candles and evergreens, not unlike an Advent wreath. She then wakes up her family with a tray of treats in her hands. This tradition remembers the candlelit visits that St. Lucia and her mother made to the poor with trays of food.

In the Kitchen

St. Lucia's Day is a traditional Scandinavian feast day, so food which originated in Scandinavia is most appropriate for this holiday. Gingersnaps are a traditional St. Lucia's Day food. There are also special buns called St. Lucia Rolls, which are made with saffron and sprinkled with raisins. Recipes for these are available online. Swedish meatballs and sweet breads can also be added to the menu.

St. Nicholas feast day is mostly celebrated in Germany and Poland, so fill the menu with German and Scandinavian foods. There is a kind of German bread specifically made for St. Nicholas's Day which is shaped like St. Nicholas. Sweet buns filled with cream cheese are a traditional St. Nicholas Day treat. Several different recipes for these can be found online.

Another special treat on St. Nicholas Day is chocolate coins, as mentioned in the *Get Creative* section. These remind us of the coins that St. Nicholas gave the three girls.

For the Very Young

If you're making a paper Jesse Tree, young children can help color in the different characters while listening to the Bible story, and they can help hang ornaments if you choose to use an evergreen tree as a Jesse Tree. Young children love learning by symbols. It's a perfect project for all ages, but especially for those who are not yet old enough to read;

the symbols of the Jesse Tree will give them visuals to accompany the Bible stories that are woven into our Advent celebrations, and can help them understand what is going on.

Advent wreaths are also a great way to involve little children in the activities of Advent. As most parents know, little children have a fascination with fire. With parental help, most toddlers would love to help light the Advent candles on the wreath. Also, if you decide to make your own Advent wreath instead of buying one, toddlers will enjoy helping decorate the greenery with the silver and gold tinsel. Including toddlers and preschoolers in the prayers and Scripture readings that accompany the lighting of the Advent candles will help them become more engaged with what is going on. They understand more than we often assume.

As an alternative to Advent *O Antiphons* (see the *Resources* section of this chapter), some people take hymns from their church's hymnal and mull over the different verses individually. Little children love to sing as well; if it's an option, singing along to familiar Advent songs such as "O Come, O Come Emmanuel" is a great way to help the young understand Advent's concepts. Even if young children can't learn the verses yet, most of them can chime in on the choruses!

St. Nicholas Day is a feast day which is especially exciting for the young. It's like a mini-Christmas: it reminds us of the even greater event which is to come. You are never too young — or too old, for that matter — to put out your shoe for "St. Nick" to fill with gifts. St. Nicholas is a wonderful role model for young children. He was the real Santa Claus, one who loved Jesus and shared that love with others.

Children love to help out in the kitchen; they can easily help make the cookies or other treats you choose to have for the St. Lucia's Day celebration.

St. Lucia's Day can also be altered to make its activities friendlier to toddlers. Sometimes a wreath of candles isn't a practical option: instead, you can have the child hold a lighted candle or even an automated candle or flashlight.

Little children love playing with small figures. Get the child a nativity scene of their own; there are many different sets which are childsafe and do not have any pieces which are small enough to choke on.

Things to Make

Jesse Tree

Advent Wreaths
St. Lucia crowns/wreaths
Jesse Tree ornaments
Advent Chains

Beyond the Home

Advent is easily celebrated outside the home by choosing to use these weeks of preparation as a time of service to others. This is the season where we remember the depth of Christ's mercy and humility in the incarnation, the Almighty God of heaven and earth as a little baby. It is a time to remember His generosity and to be generous ourselves, fulfilling our call to be servants, in imitation of Him.

Spread the joy of Advent by caroling! Go caroling up and down your street with your neighbors, or ask if you can sing outside a local department store or nursing home.

Another way to take Advent outside the home is to do a "St. Nicholas Deed," imitating the generosity of that ancient saint. On St. Nicholas Day, perhaps donate funds to charity, or put extra effort into making somebody's day special.

St. Lucia's Day can also inspire deeds of evangelism. As St. Lucia visited the poor, perhaps volunteer at a homeless shelter.

Resources

Seasonal Scripture Readings

Isaiah 9:2–7
Isaiah 11:1–9
Luke 1:5–80
John 1:1–18

Suggestions for Memorization:

Then shall the trees of the forest sing for joy before the Lord, for he comes to judge the earth. — I Chronicles 16:33

Arise, shine, for your light has come, and the glory of the Lord has risen upon you. For behold, darkness shall cover the earth, and thick darkness the peoples; but the Lord will arise upon you, and his glory will be seen upon you. And nations shall come to your light, and kings to the brightness of your rising. — *Isaiah 60:1–3*

And Mary said,
"My soul magnifies the Lord,
and my spirit rejoices in God my Savior,
for he has looked on the humble estate of his servant.
For behold, from now on all generations will call me blessed;
for he who is mighty has done great things for me,
and holy is his name.
And his mercy is for those who fear him
from generation to generation.
He has shown strength with his arm;
he has scattered the proud in the thoughts of their hearts;
he has brought down the mighty from their thrones
and exalted those of humble estate;
he has filled the hungry with good things,
and the rich he has sent away empty.
He has helped his servant Israel,
in remembrance of his mercy,
as he spoke to our fathers,
to Abraham and to his offspring forever." — *Luke 1:46–55 (The Magnificat)*

"Blessed be the Lord God of Israel,
for he has visited and redeemed his people
and has raised up a horn of salvation for us
in the house of his servant David,
as he spoke by the mouth of his holy prophets from of old,
that we should be saved from our enemies
and from the hand of all who hate us;
to show the mercy promised to our fathers
and to remember his holy covenant,
the oath that he swore to our father Abraham, to grant us
that we, being delivered from the hand of our enemies,

might serve him without fear,
in holiness and righteousness before him all our days.
And you, child, will be called the prophet of the Most High;
for you will go before the Lord to prepare his ways,
to give knowledge of salvation to his people
in the forgiveness of their sins,
because of the tender mercy of our God,
whereby the sunrise shall visit us from on high
to give light to those who sit in darkness and in the shadow of
death,
to guide our feet into the way of peace." — Luke 1:68–79 (The
Song of Zechariah)

Songs of the Season

"O Come, O Come Emmanuel," Latin, ca. 9th century.

"Savior of the Nations, Come!" Martin Luther (1483–1546), after Ambrose of Milan (340-397), translated by William M. Reynolds (1812–1876) and James Waring McCrady (born 1938).

"Lo, He Comes with Clouds Descending," Charles Wesley (1707–1788).

"Creator of the Stars of Night," Latin, 9th century.

"Come, Thou Long-Expected Jesus," Charles Wesley (1707–1788).

"Prepare the Way, O Zion," Frans Mikael Franzen (1772–1847); adapted by Charles P. Price (born 1920).

"Comfort, Comfort Ye My People," Johann G. Olearius (1611–1684).

Seasonal Reading

For Children:

The Jesse Tree, by Geraldine McCaughrean.

St. Nicholas, by Ann Tompert.

24 Days Before Christmas, by Madeline L'Engle.

Advent Storybook: 24 Stories to Share Before Christmas, by Antonie Schneider and Maja Dusikova.

The Advent Book, by Jack Stockman and Kathy Stockman.

For All Ages:
Celebrating Christmas with Jesus: an Advent Devotional, by Max Lucado.
The Advent Jesse Tree: Devotions for Children and Adults to Prepare the Coming of the Christ Child at Christmas, by Dean Lambert Smith.
The Greatest Gift: Unwrapping the Full Love Story of Christmas, by Ann Voskamp.

For More Serious Reading:
Behold, He Comes: Meditations on the Incarnation, by Benedict Groeschel, C.F.R.
God is in the Manger: Reflections on Advent, by Dietrich Bonhoeffer.
Watch for the Light, various authors, published by Orbis Books.

Prayers

Prayers and brief meditations on hymn verses are great ways to end a meal or to conclude the lighting of the Advent wreath. Here are four such prayers, one for each of the weeks of Advent:[1]

Prayer for the First Week of Advent:

> Almighty God, give us grace to cast away the works of darkness, and put on the armor of light, now in the time of this mortal life in which Your Son Jesus Christ came to visit us in great humility; that in the last day, when He shall come again in His glorious majesty to judge both the living and the dead, we may rise to the life immortal; through Him who lives and reigns with You and the Holy Spirit, one God, now and forever. *Amen.*

Prayer for the Second Week of Advent:

> Merciful God, who sent Your messengers the prophets to preach repentance and prepare the way for our salvation: give us grace to heed their warnings and forsake our sins, that we may greet with joy the coming of Jesus Christ our Redeemer; who lives and reigns with You and the Holy Spirit, one God, now and forever. *Amen.*

---

1 *Book of Common Prayer* (New York, NY: Church Publishing Incorporated, 1986), 211–212.

Prayer for the Third Week of Advent:

> Stir up Your power, O Lord, and with great might come among us; and, because we are sorely hindered by our sins, let Your bountiful grace and mercy speedily help and deliver us; through Jesus Christ our Lord, to whom, with You and the Holy Spirit, be honor and glory, now and forever. *Amen.*

Prayer for the Fourth Week of Advent:

> Purify our conscience, Almighty God, by Your daily visitation, that Your Son Jesus Christ, at His coming, may find in us a mansion prepared for Himself; who lives and reigns with You, in the unity of the Holy Spirit, one God, now and forever. *Amen.*

Repeat the prayer of the week after dinner or after lighting the Advent wreath, and perhaps follow up with a verse of an Advent hymn. The verses included in this section are from the beloved hymn, "O Come, O Come Emmanuel," and are known as the *O Antiphons.* These verses are recited or sung during the last seven days of Advent (December 17 through December 23). They have been part of the Christian church's worship since before the eighth century. Each one of these verses addresses Jesus by one of His many names (Emmanuel, Key of David, etc.). When the Latin translations of the names are arranged backwards, they spell out the Latin phrase *ero cras,* which roughly translates to "I will come tomorrow."

Antiphon for December 17:

> O come, thou Wisdom from on high, who orderest all things mightily; to us the path of knowledge show, and teach us in her ways to go. Rejoice! Rejoice! Emmanuel shall come to thee, O Israel!

Antiphon for December 18:

> O come, O come, thou Lord of might, who to thy tribes on Sinai's height in ancient times didst give the law, in cloud, and majesty, and awe. Rejoice! Rejoice! Emmanuel shall come to thee, O Israel!

Antiphon for December 19:

> O come, thou Branch of Jesse's tree, free them from Satan's

tyranny that trust thy mighty power to save, and give them victory o'er the grave. Rejoice! Rejoice! Emmanuel shall come to thee, O Israel!

Antiphon for December 20:

O come, thou Key of David, come and open wide our heavenly home; make safe the way that leads on high, and close the path to misery. Rejoice! Rejoice! Emmanuel shall come to thee, O Israel!

Antiphon for December 21:

O come, thou Dayspring from on high, and cheer us by thy drawing nigh; disperse the gloomy clouds of night, and death's dark shadow put to flight. Rejoice! Rejoice! Emmanuel shall come to thee, O Israel!

Antiphon for December 22:

O come, Desire of nations, bind in one the hearts of all mankind; bid thou our sad divisions cease, and be thyself our King of Peace. Rejoice! Rejoice! Emmanuel shall come to thee, O Israel!

Antiphon for December 23:

O come, O come Emmanuel, and ransom captive Israel, that mourns in lonely exile here until the Son of God appear. Rejoice! Rejoice! Emmanuel shall come to thee, O Israel!

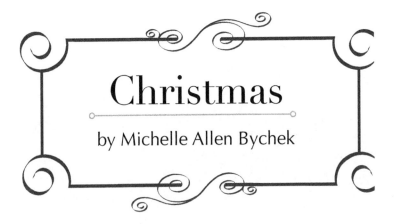

Christmas

by Michelle Allen Bychek

Introduction to Christmas

There is something exquisite about that gossamer moment when that last second of Advent ticks to completion and Christmas dawns. The raucous frenzy of the secular commercialized "Christmas" season stops on a dime and defers to the true "reason for the season." The world is silent. The cool December air seems to freeze in time, for just a moment, and the entire world holds its breath. Christ our Savior is born.

Christmas is the annual celebration of the birth of our Savior Jesus Christ to Mary, a young virgin. In traditional Christian homes, individuals and families observe Advent, a season of preparation, for four weeks prior to the Christmas celebration. Many light an Advent wreath, a circle of greens studded by candles, in anticipation of the birth of the Savior. When Christmas arrives, the Christ candle in the center of the wreath is lit to represent the birth of the Savior, and 12 days of Christmas celebration begin.

Christmas is the "Christ-Mass." It commemorates the entry of the Creator of the universe into time and human history to create mankind anew through His offer of salvation and rebirth, as spoken of in John 1:14: "And the Word became flesh and dwelt among us, and we have seen his glory, glory as of the only Son from the Father, full of grace and truth." In the incarnation, almighty God became human, affirmed the value of humanity and simultaneously embarked on an exemplary life that enables us to rise above our human nature and emulate the example of God. The single flame of a lighted Christ candle is the symbol of God become man. In the words of Jesuit poet Gerard Manley Hopkins, the incarnation is "Infinity dwindled to infancy."[1] With the incarnation, the force that formed the heavens was poured into a tiny hand and wrapped around

---

1 Gerard Manley Hopkins, *Poems and Prose* (London: Penguin Books, 1985), 55.

the forefinger of a humble human mother. He did this all because He had made us and, in spite of our fall, had looked mercifully and favorably upon us. He gave those who believe on Him "the right to become children of God" (John 1:12). It was the birth of hope. Each year, with the Christmas season, we revisit and celebrate the material birth of that hope.

The cycle of the church year allows us to experience this hope anew every 12 months. It is an annual reminder that God was with us, and is with us, in a way that we didn't expect.

Calendar

Although scholars have questioned the accuracy of the date of December 25 for the birth of Jesus, it continues to be the date of the celebration of the nativity in Western Rite Christendom. The early Christians adopted the custom of the Roman setting in which they found themselves by considering each new day to begin at one minute past midnight. Hence, in western Christian tradition Christmas begins at 12:01 a.m. on December 25.

Our current secular culture sees Christmas as a single day of celebration. However, in traditional Christian observance, Christmas isn't a single day at all. It is a season which begins on December 25 and extends a full 12 days, ending at sundown on January 5, just before the feast of the Epiphany. While Advent is a season of preparation, Christmas is a season of wonder. Celebrants have been preparing a long time for this moment; Christmas is an extended time to savor the gift.

There is some variance as to the date of Christmas between the eastern and the western churches, which is largely due to differences between the Julian and Gregorian calendars. In the 16th century, it was determined that the Julian calendar of the Romans was ten days out of synchronization, and Pope Gregory commissioned a corrected calendar. A calendar was produced which improved accuracy by changing the way leap year is calculated. It has come to be called the Gregorian calendar and was gradually adopted by most of the world. However, the Eastern Church was not in a great hurry to adopt a timekeeping system developed under the auspices of a Roman Catholic pope. As a result, many of the Eastern churches such as the Greek, Russian, Serbian, and Romanian Orthodox, continue to use the Julian calendar. For them, Christmas falls on January 6.[2]

Four significant holy days fall within the 12 days of Christmas. They are St. Stephen's Day on December 26, the feast of St. John the Apostle on December 27, the feast of the Holy Innocents on December 28, and the feast of the Holy Name of Jesus, on January 3.

The Traditions

There are many customs for the celebration of Christmas in traditional Christian homes. These holiday rituals draw family members and friends together, transmit identity and beliefs, and create memories that may be cherished. Though Christmas traditions may vary somewhat across families and cultures, the traditions covered in this section are embraced and cultivated by many Christians. (Please see the chapter on Epiphany for Twelfth Night celebrations.)

A Progressive Nativity

The static nativity scene is a familiar one in our Christmas culture: three-sided barn, Mary, Joseph, baby in manger, shepherds kneeling, wise men extending gifts, a cow, a donkey, and a single angel with wings extended. We know this scene. It is emblazoned on our consciousness.

In the traditional crèche, the manger is left empty until Christmas Eve. The figure of the baby is placed in the manger at the same time that the Christ candle is lit. Similarly, the figures of the wise men aren't placed into the nativity scene until Epiphany. Instead, they are placed at a distance from the crèche, and are moved a little closer to the stable on each of the 12 days of the Christmas season, arriving before the manger on the first day of Epiphany, January 6. This reflects the historical fact that they arrived much later than the shepherds and also the spiritual truth that we, like they, are searching to be closer to our Lord.

A nativity scene which unfolds with the story enables the individual or family to experience the story in a progressive fashion. The church year is, by its nature, a pageant. It is the annual unfolding of the gospel story, designed to be acted out in our own church and family lives. It is not static, and neither is the living crèche, or nativity scene.

The Central Candle of the Advent Wreath

The Christ candle, a white or metallic candle in the center of the Ad-

2 For more on the Julian and Gregorian calendars, see Margo Westrheim, *Celebrate: A Look at Calendars and the Ways We Celebrate* (Oxford: Oneworld Publications, 1999).

vent wreath, holds tremendous significance. It represents the incarnation. It is a physical representation of the light of life, Jesus, come into the world. It represents the dawn of new hope.

The lighting of the Christ candle is a key ritual for the transition from Advent, the season of preparation, to Christmas, the season of celebration. In many households, the tradition is for the youngest child to light the Christ candle, but, of course, anyone can light it. It is best lit in a darkened room so that the impact of the light is maximized. A singing of "O Little Town of Bethlehem" accompanies the lighting of this most significant candle nicely. A tiny votive light may be kept burning next to Mary in the crèche throughout Advent. As the Christ candle is lit, the tiny light next to Mary may be extinguished.

Nativity-Related Customs: Gift Giving

A widely kept custom on Christmas is the giving of gifts to family and friends. These gifts are reminiscent of the gifts given to Jesus by the wise men and also, the precious gift that humankind received in Jesus. Celebrants might highlight the full season by exchanging a small gift for each of the 12 days.

Reading the Story: The Nativity Narrative
People have always told stories. From cave painting on walls and ancient tales told around campfires, to medieval bards, to contemporary bedtime stories and tales of family lore, we are all about spinning a yarn. It is interesting that even in this era of social networking, people use their status updates to tell stories.

For centuries, Christians have used Christmastide to tell the story of our Savior's birth. Whether in church services, during nativity pageants, before a December fireplace, or as individuals sitting quietly while reading on a winter night, we Christians gather for the hearing of His story.

The story can be straight from the Bible, or it can be an age-appropriate abridged version. It can come from any version of the Bible. It can even be a picture book, or someone's paraphrase. It is the (accurate) telling that is important.

One of the things that seals traditions and makes them meaningful is ritual. Ritual is built by repetition and order. We are creatures of habit, so repetition and order speak to us. Reading the story on a certain night each Christmas season, at a certain time, or in a certain place can help solidify tradition. Reading a certain version of the story, even if it is a bit longer or more detailed than the youngest ones can process may be beneficial. Luke 2:1–20 is a good choice. There is plenty of time during the Christmas season for kid-friendly versions of the story. But, one night out of the 12 days of Christmas, the family might benefit from being immersed in the rhythms of pure Scripture, unadulterated by attempts at simplification. Give the little ones a cup of hot cocoa, sit them on laps, and allow them to be warmed inside and out by the fire's glow and the Spirit's presence. They will sit, and they will listen. Their hearts will hear and each year they will grow in understanding.

Christmas Trees and Christian Monogram Ornaments
The Christmas tree is the central symbol of Christmas for many people. Ornament-clad artificial trees begin popping up in stores right after Halloween. These glitzy and often theme-based trees, with their plastic renditions of cola-drinking Santas, cartoon characters, gleaming glass balls, and flashing colored lights, seem to bear little relationship to the infant Christ. Why, then, are they such a central element of the celebration?

Pine trees, the traditional choice for Christmas trees and a familiar symbol of winter, are green all year. They seem eternal. During the short days of the coldest season, when things seem most desolate, these trees wear emerald all year, and speak of life. They are the ever-present promise of the advent of spring.

The evergreen tree has represented life in the dead of winter for at least 1000 years, across cultures. To Christians, it is a living symbol of the new life and hope born on Christmas. They announce the birth of Christ that was to usher in, for us, the gift of eternal life. They are a worthy symbol of the season.

One of the ways to emphasize the Christian hope represented by the evergreen tree is through decoration with Christian symbols. The introduction of the concept of Christian monograms (or "Chrismons") as tree decorations is attributable to Frances Kipps Spencer, in the late 1940s, at Ascension Lutheran Church in Danville, Virginia. These decorations are usually white with gold trim, and sometimes a small amount of red. They are based on various ancient Christian symbols including crosses, the *chi rho*, the anchor, the fish, and others.

Decorating the tree with these symbols invests greater depth to the Christmas tree in the home. One approach is to make a new symbol, have a short lesson on its meaning, and add it to the tree on each of the 12 days of Christmas. Christian monogram ornaments can be crafted at home with various materials and techniques including felt, beads, cross-stitch, or needlepoint.

First Gifts on Christmas Eve
The tradition of opening one gift each on Christmas Eve helps to keep the focus on the arrival of Jesus as the reason for gift-giving. After all, Jesus was the single greatest gift that anyone has ever received.

The Christmas Dinner with Table Blessings
Christmas dinner is a central event of the season. It often involves a gathering of extended family and friends, and extensive preparations. These are things that make it wonderful. These are also things that can spell stress. That stress might be minimized by beginning the meal with a Scripture reading and prayer appropriate to the ages of the participants.

Midnight Mass and Christmas Day Worship
For Christians, Christmas worship is inseparable from Christmas celebration. The time and content of the service attended is often determined by the age of the attendees, and family tradition. Families with young children may go to a Christmas Eve service in the evening. Adults may attend a midnight mass. For many people, the Christmas morning worship service is the norm. However, the practice of celebrating three Christmas masses is an ancient one. The early Jerusalem church attended mass at midnight at the grotto of the Nativity in Bethlehem. They subsequently returned to Jerusalem and met at dawn for a second mass at the Basilica of the Resurrection. Later in the day, they attended regular worship services.

Today, services held at various times of day still each have unique character. Midnight mass is the first proclamation of the birth of the King and is an opportunity to focus on the birth of Jesus in our hearts and souls. We savor the feeling of peace and holiness as we kneel at the crib of our Savior. Celebrating Christmas at dawn ties the birth of Christ to His eventual resurrection; it is a time to focus on Jesus as true God and true man. Christmas Day services are festive and gather the whole church in jubilant celebration of the fact that Jesus became man that we might become sons of God.

Handel's Messiah

On August 22, 1791, George Frideric Handel set to work on a new three-act *oratorio*. This *oratorio* was to tell the story of the most significant happenings in the life of Christ: His birth, the redemption story, and His resurrection and future kingdom on earth. The Christmas portion took seven days to complete. The remaining portions required another 12 days. The new work was titled *Messiah*.

Performances were packed. At the second performance, King George II was so moved by the piece that he stood during the Hallelujah chorus. In keeping with proper etiquette in the presence of royalty and the strong impact of the work, all other theater-goers followed suit. Word spread, and the practice continued for all subsequent performances, as it does to this day.[3]

It has become a widespread tradition to attend performances of Handel's *Messiah* at Christmastime. Often, performances are a benefit for a charitable cause. *Messiah* is an excellent way to keep one's perspective on the place of the incarnation in a glorious and powerful story of God reaching down to His creation with the priceless gift of redemption.

St. Stephen's Day (Boxing Day)

Publicly-recognized saints are historical figures of significance in the church, and they are remembered for their heroic faith and actions as followers of our Lord Jesus Christ. They may serve as examples for us and our children. St. Stephen is one such saint. As the first Christian martyr (Acts 6:1–8:3), he stands as a beacon of faith and charity. Tradition holds that Stephen was stoned to death on December 26. At the time of his death, he asked God to forgive those who threw the stones.

The celebration of St. Stephen's Day finds its origins in the Middle Ages, when alms boxes were present in all churches. Throughout the year, the faithful were encouraged to place offerings for the poor in these boxes (hence the name "Boxing Day"), which were not unlocked until St. Stephen's Day. In memory of St. Stephen, priests distributed the contents to the poorest of the poor, in honor of his generous spirit. Similarly, on this day throughout England during the Middle Ages, the wealthy distributed boxes of gifts and treats to those who provided household service throughout the year. Persons in service eventually

---

3 For more on the history of Handel's *Messiah*, and its relationship to the Christmas season, see: Ace Collins, *Stories Behind the Great Traditions of Christmas* (Grand Rapids, MI: Zondervan, 2003).

came to bring their own boxes to the homes of their wealthy employers to be filled.

Christian individuals and families may benefit greatly from cherishing and expanding this tradition within the context of their own homes and lives. Traditions include working in a soup kitchen on this day, distributing to the poor toys that are no longer used, and giving a special gift to a charity that provides for the needs of the disadvantaged.

Feast of St. John, Apostle

December 27, the third day of Christmas, is also the feast day of St. John the Apostle and Evangelist. John was the only disciple to stand faithfully by Jesus in the hour of His passion. As he stood at the foot of the cross, he was named by our Lord to be the guardian of Jesus' mother, Mary. In his writings, John gave us a treasure of expressions of Christian love. It is appropriate to read a portion of John's gospel or one of his epistles for family devotions on this day. The reading might be accompanied by special mulled wine or cider and a toast to St. John's love (see the *In the Kitchen* section of this chapter).

Holy Innocents

December 28 is the feast day of the Holy Innocents, the children slaughtered by King Herod following the birth of Jesus. Both the contemporaneous historical records of Josephus and the writings of modern day scholars assure us that King Herod was not a nice guy. He is widely understood to have exhibited depression, anxiety, and paranoia, to which he reacted with bouts of violence. He is known to have had family members and many rabbis killed. He had a tendency to do away with people whom he thought might usurp his power.

Accordingly, when he was visited by the wise men from the East and told of the new King who had been born, his paranoia went into overdrive. When the magi wisely chose not to return to inform him of the whereabouts of the child, he acted on this paranoia by ordering a slaughter of all firstborn infants in the kingdom. Those innocent babes are remembered on the Feast of the Holy Innocents, also called *Childermas* or Children's Mass, on December 28.

Like St. Stephen's Day, on which Boxing Day falls, Holy Innocents is a solemn occasion. It is a foreshadowing of the persecution of Christians that was to come, and, to some extent, of the crucifixion.

This day can be used in the home to focus upon the gift of children. It is an ideal day for parents to pray for and bless their children.

It is also a good day to teach about the historical persecution of Christians, as well as modern day examples of this evil.

Holy Name

Eight days after birth, Jewish babies were circumcised and given a name. In remembrance of those events, and with respect to the centrality of the name of Jesus in Christian life and worship, we celebrate the feast of the Holy Name of Jesus. There is some variance among western rite churches as to the date of the feast. It is celebrated on January 1 in most Protestant traditions. The holy name of Jesus is traditionally associated with the Christogram "IHS" in the western church. The acronym "IHS" is an ancient abbreviation for the name of Jesus in Greek and has been in use in the western church to represent the Savior for centuries. It denotes the first three letters of the Greek name of Jesus: iota-eta-sigma or IHΣ. It has also been interpreted in the west as standing for "Jesus, Savior of men" (in Latin).

Names had great significance in the middle-eastern culture of Jesus' day. Jesus' name means "The Lord Saves." We are told that at the name of Jesus, "every knee should bow" (Philippians 2:10), and we are commanded to pray in the name of our Lord Jesus Christ. It is the practice of many traditional liturgical Christians to bow, or at least tip their heads, when the name of Jesus is spoken by themselves or others.

There are many ways to observe the Feast of the Holy Name. This is a good day to repent of times that the name of Jesus has been used irreverently. It is also a good day to teach children about the Christogram "IHS." Perhaps one of the best is to meditate upon how we might better do all things in the coming year in His name and to His glory.

Get Creative

While all of the neighbors are taking the tree to the curb and unstringing the lights, keeping the focus on Christmas joy for the full 12 days of the season can feel a little countercultural. In traditional observance, though, the Christmas tree and other household decorations related to the season are kept up for the full 12 days of Christmas in order to fully celebrate the long-awaited and joy-filled holiday.

In the Christian home, the Christmas tradition of gift-giving can be extended to include charitable giving. The family might make a special trip to the store to purchase items for a specific shelter or collect items from throughout the home to be donated. The focus on giving might also be extended to the neighborhood.

On each of the 12 days of Christmas, establish a hope, wish, goal, or priority for one of the 12 months of the coming year.

Add a special decoration to the tree on each day of the season.

Take a cue from German tradition and save the decoration of the tree for Christmas Eve.

Change all of the candles in the Advent wreath to white on Christmas morning to highlight the arrival of hope and light them all on each of the 12 days of the season.

Choose a family in the neighborhood, church, school or workplace for each of the 12 days. Deliver a small food gift to that family with a note attached stating, "Happy second (or third or fourth, etc.) day of Christmas!"

While most of the world is wrapping each figurine of the nativity set in newspaper and packing it away, why not use the 12 days of Christmas to really think about the nativity story and its aftermath? Focus on one element each day:

First Day of Christmas: The Christ Child has arrived! Meditate on this remarkable gift of grace.

Second Day of Christmas: Today is the feast day of St. Stephen, the first Christian martyr. Obviously, St. Stephen took God's gift of His Son seriously. Have we allowed the depth of the gift to really sink in?

Third Day of Christmas: Today is the feast day of St. John, the Apostle. St. John was "the disciple whom Jesus loved." He held a special place in Jesus' heart. Take time on this day to remember that we are all loved by the Savior, who has called us His own.

Fourth Day of Christmas: The Holy Innocents, and their parents, paid a tremendous price. Focus this day on the gift of children, and on how the suffering of children in today's world might be lifted in some small way by your actions.

Fifth Day of Christmas: The humble shepherds were the first to arrive. God chose to announce the arrival of His son to the lowly. Consider what it means that the angels announced the message of glad tidings for *all people*.

Sixth Day of Christmas: Joseph was an ordinary blue-collar tradesman. He was a just man called to a huge responsibility.

When God calls us to reach beyond our comfort zones and accomplish something for Him, are we ready and willing, as Joseph was?

Seventh Day of Christmas: Mary was an innocent young girl from a rural town. Yet she was called to be the mother of God. She must have been afraid, and yet, she trusted. Do we have such total trust in God?

Eighth Day of Christmas: Today is the feast day of the Holy Name of Jesus. We are taught that "at the name of Jesus every knee should bow," and that we are to do all things in the name of Christ Jesus. How might we make a special effort to stay true to these callings in the coming year?

Ninth Day of Christmas: The baby Jesus was laid in a manger. It is hardly the accommodations that we would deem suitable. Perhaps it is a lesson to us, that great things may not be where we expect to find them. Where can you find grace this holiday season, in unexpected places?

Tenth Day of Christmas: The heavenly hosts burst forth with spontaneous celebratory song. Imagine the joy. Are we so accustomed to the annual celebration of the incarnation that we have lost sight of the depth of joy that it inspired in the angels?

Eleventh Day of Christmas: King Herod believed that his paltry human efforts would stay the hand of God. Absurd, right? How do we fight against the will of God in our lives?

Twelfth Day of Christmas: We tend to picture the wise men leaning over the manger gazing upon the infant Christ. The truth is, they searched long and traveled far to meet the Savior. Are we searching? How far are we willing to go to find Him?

Around the World

Although it is not formally celebrated in the United States as an official holiday, Boxing Day is observed in most English-speaking countries. During the reign of Queen Victoria, St. Stephen's Day, complete with its traditions of charity in memory of St. Stephen who showed such charity at the time of his martyrdom, was codified as an official holiday in the United Kingdom.

In Australia, Christmas falls in the summertime. This allows for the popularity of outdoor activities to celebrate the season. A particularly popular activity is Carols by Candlelight, during which people gather at night to light candles and sing carols under the night sky.

Members of the Christian community in China decorate their Christmas trees with paper lanterns, red paper chains, and flowers. They place red paper pagodas in the windows symbolizing happiness.

In Italy, the center of Christmas celebrations is the crib, or manger scene. Families gather at the crib for each of the nine days before Christmas for prayer. On Christmas Eve, they pass the baby Jesus figure from person to person before placing it lovingly into the crib.

In the Kitchen

Christmas Cookies: One of the best known Christmas food traditions is, of course, Christmas cookies. Many a Christmas memory includes rolling pins, cookie cutters, and candy sprinkles. Including stars, mangers, angels, and nativity scene figures can help keep the focus on the birthday of the King.

Hot Drinks: The birth of Jesus shines warmth upon a long and dark departing season of waiting. Hot drinks have long been part of the celebration of the return of light and warmth. Eggnog, spiced cider, and wassail punch (with or without alcohol!) are key traditional hot drinks of the season and can add warmth to a family gathering before a crackling log in the fireplace.

Fruitcake: Fruitcake is the proverbial joke of the Christmas season. Why is fruitcake associated with Christmas? Although the use of dried fruits, nuts, and honey in cakes is an ancient practice, our traditional Christmas fruitcake can be traced back to the Middle Ages. Dried fruits were an expensive import, reserved for special times. The process of making a fruitcake was very labor intensive – and still is, to a degree. Fruitcakes differ from other types of cakes in that they keep a long time and can be sent over distances to loved ones without spoiling. Fruitcake was a special delicacy for friends and family and was a prized Christmas gift. Folks who are not great lovers of fruitcake can still give a nod to the tradition by making a quick bread that contains a bit of dried fruit.

Cinnamon Rolls: Christmas morning in many childhood homes meant cinnamon rolls. They can be a warm, sweet, spiced start to a very special day. Preparing the dough the night before and allowing it to rise overnight in the refrigerator makes Christmas morning a cinch.

Gingerbread: It is uncertain whether gingerbread houses originated with the publication of the tale of Hansel and Gretel by the Brothers Grimm in the 1800s or whether they were writing about something that already existed. However, the association of gingerbread houses with Christmas is a strong one. Why not expand the tradition to include the making of a gingerbread nativity scene?

St John's Love: In old tradition, wine was blessed on St. John's Day in the churches. Legend has it that St. John once drank wine that had been poisoned. However, he did not die, because he had blessed the wine first. Of course, it was John's faith that saved him. It is tradition in some parts of the world to drink "St. John's Love" on this night. St. John's Love can simply be blessed wine, but warmed spiced wine is a special treat. Partakers of this mulled wine drink to the "love of St. John."

St. John's Love

Ingredients
- 1 bottle of red wine
- 2–3 whole cloves
- 2–3 cinnamon sticks
- 1–2 cardamom seeds
- ¼–½ tsp. nutmeg
- sugar to taste

Method
1. Warm a bottle of red wine over the stove.
2. Add cloves, cinnamon sticks, cardamom, nutmeg, and sugar.
3. Boil for 4–6 minutes.
4. Strain out the spices and serve while hot.

Stollen: Many of us have heard of the German sweet bread called stollen. This bread is shaped to resemble the swaddling clothes of baby

Jesus, then covered with a thin white sugar frosting. It is a special remembrance of the infant Jesus during the Christmas season.

For the Very Young

Jesus' birthday cake: Though the baking of a cake seems a natural response to a birthday celebration, the tradition of baking a birthday cake for Jesus in probably only a few hundred years old, and appears to have begun in Germany. In the 1800s, the tradition began to spread to England and America. Recently, as Christians have increased the emphasis on Jesus as "the reason for the season," the practice of baking a birthday cake for Jesus has become increasingly popular. It can be especially beneficial for homes with children, as it helps to explain the true meaning of Christmas through a familiar rite of birthday celebration. When combined with the singing of "Happy Birthday," the serving of cake helps to highlight, especially for children, that a birthday celebration is taking place. This ritual can take place on Christmas Eve, after the baby is placed in the manger of the family's nativity scene, and may be combined with the opening of the "first gift" for each family member.

Lollipop Angel: Cover the round part of the lollipop with tissue paper and pull it down over the stick to make a dress. Tie a piece of yarn, string, or ribbon over the tissue, below the "head." Use a marker to draw a face. Add to the dress with more tissue paper, and/or yarn, if desired. Use more tissue paper, construction paper, and/or pipe cleaners to make wings. Glue the wings to the angel. Use glitter glue to decorate, if desired.

Popsicle Stick Nativity: Glue popsicle sticks to a sheet of paper to create the basic outline of a barn. Use crayons to draw the figures in the nativity scene. Now that Christmas has arrived, be sure to include baby Jesus!

Jesus Paper Chain: Cut out small rectangular pieces of paper. Write a letter on each as follows: one *J*, one *E*, two *S*'s, and one *U* for each segment of the chain. Help little ones make a paper chain by making paper rings and joining them together to spell Jesus. Paper rings can be secured using tape or glue stick. Long paper chains make a great addition to the tree.

Jesus Banners: Write out the name of Jesus in block letters on heavy paper. Use glue and sequins, glitter, crayons, paint, etc. to decorate. Allow to dry completely and then hang.

Holy Name Sugar Cookies: On the Feast of the Holy Name of Jesus, families might also make sugar cookies and cut them into the letters *I*, *H*, and *S*.

Acting Out the Nativity Story: Children love to play-act; let them act out the nativity story! They can don their dress-up clothes and play the characters or use puppets to tell the story, but either way, getting in character and reciting the words of the story will help the good news of Jesus' incarnation sink into their minds and hearts.

Things to Make

Scented Cinnamon-Applesauce Ornaments: Mix 2 cups cinnamon with 2 cups applesauce. Add one teaspoon ground cloves and/or one teaspoon nutmeg, if desired. You should have wet, but firm, dough that will hold its shape when formed. If needed, add more applesauce for moisture, or more spices for dryness, until the dough is an appropriate consistency. Up to two teaspoons of white glue can be added, if needed, to enable dough to hold its shape. Roll or flatten the mixture to the desired thickness for ornaments. Cut with cookie cutters. Nativity cutters make an excellent choice.

Christian Monogram Ornaments: Print out Christian symbol templates from the internet or copy them from a book. A computer search for "Christian Monograms" or "Chrismons" should reveal Internet sources. Cut the symbols out. Choose a symbol, turn it upside down, and place it atop a white foam sheet from the craft store. Cut around the symbol with a pair of scissors, or a craft knife. Cut a hole for a ribbon hanger. Be absolutely certain that children have adequate supervision, and that the tools they use are safe and developmentally appropriate. Remove the symbol from the sheet and paint the top of it with sparkle decoupage glue-sealer. Decorate with glitter glue. When dry, tie a ribbon hanger into the hole.

Orange and Clove Christmas Pomander: To make a Christmas orange pomander, you'll need a navel orange, a toothpick, whole cloves, and a length of ribbon. Cross-tie the ribbon on the orange by centering the ribbon over the orange, wrapping it around in a north-south fashion until it meets at the bottom. Cross the ribbon at the bottom and pull tight against the orange. Then wrap it around the orange in an east-west fashion until it meets at the top (like wrapping a present with ribbon). Tie the ribbon securely at the top. Then, insert cloves into the orange. It will be easier to insert them if you poke a hole in the orange peel first with a toothpick. You can either create a design with the cloves, or cover the whole orange. Then, wrap the clove covered orange with velvet ribbon as desired, pinning it in place if necessary. Hang in your home. If the orange is completely covered in cloves, the ornament will last much longer. Kids will enjoy making simpler designs and leaving significant portions of the orange to show through. You'll want plenty of paper towels around. This craft can get juicy.

Twelve ideas for symbols are included here, to provide at least one for each of the 12 days of Christmas:

Fish: An ancient symbol of Christ.

Crown: Symbolizes the kingship of our Lord.

Anchor Cross: A symbol of our hope rooted in Christ.

Five Pointed Star: Symbolizes the manifestation of Christ.

Crown of Thorns: Foreshadows the atonement.

Descending Dove: Represents the Holy Spirit at our Lord's baptism.

Trefoil: Represents the Holy Trinity.

Jerusalem Cross: Represents the five wounds of our Lord's crucifixion.

Lamb: An ancient and enduring symbol of our Lord, the Lamb of God.

Alpha and Omega: A symbol of Jesus' divinity.

Chi Rho: A symbol of Jesus the Christ.

Shell: Symbolizes baptism.

Beyond the Home

Jesus was born into very humble circumstances. The King of kings lay in an animal feeder among beasts of the field. Children of God find themselves is equally humble circumstances throughout the world today. Honor Jesus on His birthday by giving a gift to improve the circumstances of some of these children. For example, your household may choose to provide mosquito nets to prevent the spread of malaria or clean drinking water to children in developing countries. Domestically, one might give the gift of time to children without a healthy, intact family.

In keeping with the Christmas tradition of gift-giving, families or individuals might choose one or more families to extend a special kindness to or perform a special service for. Children will delight in leaving a special handmade gift on a neighbor's doorstep, ringing the bell, and running! A special service day on which time is donated to the church for cleaning, yard work, or some other useful service might also be a blessing.

The secular Christmas season is awash with a focus on the modern Santa Claus. What of the true St. Nicholas, though? A favorite tale of the historic St. Nicholas, bishop of Myra, tells of his efforts to save three young girls, who lived in poverty, from a horrible fate (see the *Advent* chapter for the full story). The spirit of the true St. Nicholas can be celebrated during the 12 days of Christmas by setting some money aside to give to a charity that combats human trafficking and saves girls from its clutches. One way to do this is to fast from one or more meals on the Feast of the Holy Innocents and give the money saved on food to such an organization.

On Holy Innocents' Day (December 28), the household might choose a victim of modern-day persecution, such as a Christian that is currently jailed for his or her faith somewhere in the world, and pray for that individual. It is also a good day to make and deliver homemade items, such as blankets, to a children's hospital or battered women and children's shelter.

Resources

Seasonal Scripture Readings

Nativity Story: Luke 2:1–20[4]
St. Stephen: Acts 6:8–7:2a, 7:51–60
I John 1:1–9
Massacre of the Holy Innocents: Matthew 2:13–18

---

4 Readings are from the Episcopal form of the *Revised Common Lectionary*.

Suggestions for Memorization

And in the same region there were shepherds out in the field, keeping watch over their flock by night. And an angel of the Lord appeared to them, and the glory of the Lord shone around them, and they were filled with great fear. And the angel said to them, "fear not, for behold, I bring you good news of great joy that will be for all people. For unto you is born this day in the city of David a Savior, who is Christ the Lord. And this will be a sign for you: you will find a baby wrapped in swaddling cloths and lying in a manger." — Luke 2:8–12

"Behold, the virgin shall conceive and bear a son, and they shall call his name Immanuel" (which means, God with us). — Matthew 1:23

And this is the testimony, that God gave us eternal life, and this life is in his Son. Whoever has the Son has life; whoever does not have the Son of God does not have life. — I John 5:11–12

Songs of the Season

"Joy to the World," original by Isaac Watts, 1719.
"Holy Night," Adolphe Adam,1847.
"The First Noel," current version by William B. Sandys, 1823.
"Hark the Herald Angels Sing," Charles Wesley, 1839.

Seasonal Reading

For Children:
Christmas in the Manger Board Book, by Nola Buck.
This is the Stable, by Cynthia Cotton.
Room for a Little One: A Christmas Tale, by Martin Waddell.

For All Ages:

The Life of Our Lord, by Charles Dickens. The story of the life of Jesus based on Luke's gospel. Written for his children, and allowed to be published only after the death of his last living child.

Christmas in the Big Woods, by Laura Ingalls Wilder.

The Christmas Miracle of Jonathan Toomey, by Susan Wojciechowski. The heartwarming story of the life changing impact of the Christmas story on a hurting and bitter man.

For More Serious Reading:

On The Incarnation of the Word, by St. Athanasius.

Prayers

Collects for The Nativity of Our Lord: Christmas Day

O God, you make us glad by the yearly festival of the birth of your only Son Jesus Christ: Grant that we, who joyfully receive him as our Redeemer, may with sure confidence behold him when he comes to be our Judge; who lives and reigns with you and the Holy Spirit, one God, now and for ever. Amen.

- or this -

O God, you have caused this holy night to shine with the brightness of the true Light: Grant that we, who have known the mystery of that Light on earth, may also enjoy him perfectly in heaven; where with you and the Holy Spirit he lives and reigns, one God, in glory everlasting. Amen.

- or this -

Almighty God, you have given your only-begotten Son to take our nature upon him, and to be born [this day] of a pure virgin: Grant that we, who have been born again and made your children by adoption and grace, may daily be renewed by your Holy Spirit; through our Lord Jesus Christ, to whom with you and the same Spirit be honor and glory, now and for ever. Amen.[5]

Christmas Dinner Prayer

Ah, dearest Jesus, holy Child,

---

5 *The Book of Common Prayer* (1986), 212–213.

Make thee a bed, soft, undefiled,
Within my heart, that it may be
A quiet chamber kept for Thee.

My heart for very joy doth leap,
My lips no more can silence keep,
I too must sing, with joyful tongue,
That sweetest ancient song,

Glory to God in highest heaven,
Who unto man His Son hath given
While angels sing with pious mirth.
A glad new year to all the earth!
— Martin Luther[6]

---

6 Attributed to Martin Luther, 1483–1546, PD/1923.

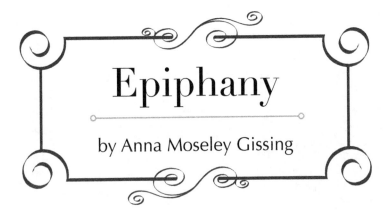

Epiphany

by Anna Moseley Gissing

Introduction to Epiphany

For many, Epiphany may come and go without notice. In our current American culture, the "holiday season" from October through December can induce a post-holiday coma — too much sugar, too much noise, too many activities, and too much spending. If we are carried along by this pattern year after year, Epiphany may be an afterthought that never quite gets "thought."

Even those who have some sense of wanting to observe the church calendar may find themselves skipping from Christmas to Lent without a second thought. Yet if you have been observing Advent as a time of preparation and have been celebrating Christmas for 12 days, Epiphany will naturally follow.

For some, observing some parts of the church calendar seems odd or even, frankly, wrong. Though days like Christmas and Easter are clearly connected to their narratives in scripture, other days "aren't in the Bible." Epiphany is one of those times we can miss if we don't connect this season with its purpose and its place in the gospel story. Indeed, Epiphany connects Christ's birth and incarnation, celebrated at Christmas, with His preparation for death on the cross.

In between the stories of Christmas and Easter, the gospels tell us of Jesus' earthly life and ministry. Epiphany is a fitting time to reflect on this life. Jesus wasn't just born and then crucified. In this season, we reflect on the "meantime."

The word "epiphany" comes from the Greek word *epiphaneia* which means "manifestation" or "revelation" and is derived from the verb "to reveal" or "to make manifest." All four of the major scriptural events celebrated during Epiphany — the visit of the magi, the presentation of Jesus at the temple, His baptism, and His first miracle at the wedding in Cana — are *manifestations* of God's glory in the person

43

of Jesus Christ.

Epiphany is the perfect word for this season in which God reveals Himself to the magi, leading them to Jesus with a star. This remarkable account is in Matthew 2. Who are these magi? We're not quite sure. Some say they were astrologers or astronomers since they noticed the new star. Some call them kings (as in the familiar song). The text does not give us much to describe them. However, we do know they were "from the east" and therefore foreigners. They did not know the Scriptures. In a word, they were Gentiles. Yet, God reveals to them a star, and they follow that star in order to worship Jesus, "born King of the Jews" (2:2). What a beautiful example of the gospel! People from far away are drawn in to worship the King of the Jews. The good news of Jesus is not only for the Jews but indeed for the whole world. Epiphany celebrates this manifestation of God to the world.

Though the New Testament does not give us much information about the magi, traditions have developed about them in the church over the centuries. By convention, there were three kings, and their names were Caspar, Melchior, and Balthasar. We do know that there was more than one, and they came to worship bringing three gifts. All of these gifts were fit to give a king. And these gifts are spiritually symbolic as well, representing roles of Jesus: gold for His Kingship; frankincense, His divinity; and myrrh, a symbol of His death to come. In the gifts alone we have a foreshadowing of Jesus' life.[1]

With the birth of Jesus, the Kingdom of God breaks into the world in a new way, as indeed Jesus proclaims in his earthly ministry. In Matthew 2, we see this breaking in of the Kingdom. These magi are a foretaste of the "latter days" described in Micah 4 and Isaiah 2 where peoples from many nations will come to worship the Lord. This is a glimpse of the Kingdom of God, on earth as it will be in the future.

Epiphany celebrates this manifestation of glory to the magi (and to the Gentiles generally). The presence of Jesus was revealed to them through the light of a star. And this season has an emphasis on light as well. Jesus is the light of the world (see John 8 and 9). But Jesus shines light on His disciples. And now, we (His followers) are the light of the world (Matt. 5). Epiphany is about the manifestation and revelation that Jesus is the light, and the call to make that light known to other people.

The visit of the magi is the focus of western observance of Epiph-

---

1 J. C. J. Metford, *The Christian Year* (New York, NY: Crossroad, 1991), 41.

any. In eastern churches, the baptism of Jesus is the focus, and the feast is known as *theophany*. Like *epiphany*, the word *theophany* means "revelation" or "manifestation," only this revelation or manifestation is clearly of God. At His baptism, Jesus' identity as the Son of God is made manifest as God declares His pleasure with His Son (see Matt. 3:13–17). Just as God sent a star to lead the magi to worship Jesus, God later opened the heavens, declaring His pleasure with His own Son to those at the Jordan River. In the west, Jesus' baptism is generally celebrated the Sunday after Epiphany.

Another important gospel narrative remembered during Epiphany is Jesus' miracle at the wedding at Cana. In John 2 we learn that when the wine ran out at a wedding, Jesus turned water into wine. In this first miracle, Jesus "manifested his glory" (2:11) revealing a bit more of his identity. And as a result, his disciples believed in Him.

On February 2, we celebrate the presentation of the Lord at the temple. Also called Candlemas, this day — 40 days past Christmas — observes the narrative in Luke 2:22–38, in which Jesus is presented to God as a first-born son and Mary is purified 40 days after giving birth, according to the Mosaic law. There Jesus, Joseph, and Mary encounter Simeon and Anna, who both praise and thank God for bringing redemption and revelation to the people of Israel. This is another manifestation of Jesus' identity. In the words of Simeon, he is "a light for revelation to the Gentiles, and for glory to your people Israel" (Luke 2:32). Candles lit on this day in particular celebrate this light Jesus who has been made manifest to us.[2]

On the final Sunday before Ash Wednesday, some western traditions celebrate the transfiguration, described in Luke 9:28–36 (and also Matt. 17:1–8; Mark 9:2–8). The transfiguration is a powerful scene of God's glory shining forth as Jesus becomes dazzling white and Moses and Elijah appear as well. Here again, God reveals that Jesus is His Son. Yet another revelation of Jesus' identity and glory is recorded in this narrative. And we have another Sunday to celebrate this glory and manifestation just days before Lent begins.[3]

After we have prepared to welcome Christ during Advent and

---

2 Adolf Adam, *The Liturgical Year* (New York, NY: Pueblo Publishing Company, 1981), 149–152.

3 Bobby Gross describes this placement of Transfiguration Sunday in *Living the Christian Year* (Downer's Grove, IL: InterVarsity Press, 2009), 86. (Other traditions celebrate it on August 6; for more information, please see the chapter on Ordinary Time.)

indeed have welcomed Him during Christmas, Epiphany gives us the opportunity to tell the world about Him. The Light has come into the world and it is our time to share that light with others. This oft-overlooked season is important since it reminds us to respond to the gift of Christ's incarnation and to speak about the light of Christ in an intentional way. Jesus, though born King of the Jews, is also King of the world. The gospel breaks down barriers between Jews and Gentiles and indeed all kinds of barriers in our own lives, uniting rich and poor, young and old, male and female, black and white, under King Jesus. Let us show forth the light of God's glory.

Calendar

Epiphany is January 6, and Twelfth Night celebrates this move from Christmas to Epiphany. Some consider Twelfth Night part of Christmas, but many follow the Jewish practice of recognizing the beginning of a day with sundown the evening before. (Note this reckoning: "And there was evening and there was morning" in Gen. 1.) Therefore, Epiphany would begin on the eve of January 6. Some only celebrate the feast day of Epiphany on January 6 and then follow Ordinary Time[4] until Ash Wednesday, but others celebrate the season for the five to nine weeks between January 6 and Ash Wednesday. Because Easter is a moveable feast, Ash Wednesday moves in conjunction with Easter and Lent, making the length and end of Epiphany variable.

There are several other important dates in Epiphany. The baptism of Jesus is commemorated on the Sunday after January 6 and the presentation of the Lord at the Temple on February 2. In Reformed tradition, the Sunday before Ash Wednesday is celebrated as Transfiguration Sunday. Finally, Shrove Tuesday is celebrated on the very last day of Epiphany, just before the season of Lent begins.

The Traditions

Twelfth Night

It is traditional to celebrate the end of Christmastide and beginning of Epiphany with a Twelfth Night party on the night of January 5. This festivity celebrates the light of the world and sharing that light with

---

4 For more about Ordinary Time, please see chapter 8.

others.

A central part of the Twelfth Night party is the Twelfth Night Cake, sometimes called the King Cake. There are many variations on this cake, which is most often a spiced cake. It is sometimes baked in the shape of a ring and sometimes more like a standard fruit cake. Usually, something is inserted in the cake: a bean, a pea, or a plastic baby. According to tradition, whoever finds the bean or baby is the Twelfth Night "king." The king will rule over the party. If there is also a pea inserted, the one who finds the pea will be the queen. These two will act out their rule over the evening festivities and may also be responsible for hosting the party the following year[5] or just for baking and bringing next year's King Cake.

Another part of the Twelfth Night party is the reversal of social roles for the night. This tradition doesn't seem to be Christian in origin, but it is true that the Kingdom of God that Jesus ushers in is one full of paradox and of role reversal: Jesus, the King of the Jews, dies for the salvation of the world instead of fighting for political power. He spends time with "sinners" instead of cozying up to the religious leaders. He teaches that His followers need to be prepared to lose their lives in order to gain them. This is role reversal at its best.[6]

Magi Arrive

If there is a nativity scene in the home, the magi may have been making their way to the manger throughout Christmastide. On Epiphany, they finally arrive at the manger and the "scene" is complete. If there are children around, let them be the ones who carry the magi to their destination. Once there, read their story in Matthew 2 and talk about how God guided them to Jesus. Allowing the magi to travel around the house towards Jesus keeps the gospel story central during Christmastide and into Epiphany.

Decorations

The first day of Epiphany is also a traditional day for taking down Christmas decorations. Though many others strip their decorations on December 26, celebrating Christmastide ensures a festive house even longer. As you straighten up from the Twelfth Night celebration, why

5 Lauren Winner, *A Cheerful and Comfortable Faith* (New Haven, CT: Yale University Press, 2010), 129–135, and Metford, *The Christian Year*, 41–42.
6 See Winner, *Cheerful*, 129–135 for more on this.

not make it a joyful time of taking down and putting away Christmas decorations? You may want to leave up some strings of lights or electric candles in the windows though to symbolize this "light of the world."

Blessing of Homes

Another convention of Epiphany is the blessing of homes. Most practice this blessing by chalking the outside of the door frame with the formula 20 + C + M + B + 12 (if it were, in fact, 2012). This cryptic symbol simply stands for the year and the traditional names of the magi: Caspar, Melchior, and Balthasar. The letters CMB also serve as an acronym for "May Christ bless this house" in Latin (*Christus mansionem benedicat*). As you write these symbols around your door, say a prayer for God to bless your home, your family, and those who enter.

Gifts

Since Epiphany celebrates the day the magi arrived to present gifts to Jesus, it is appropriate to symbolize this narrative with gift-giving. In some homes, gifts are opened on Epiphany instead of, or in addition to, Christmas Day. You may choose to wait until January 6 to open some or all of the Christmas gifts as a way to celebrate this day when the magi gave gifts to Jesus. Following the example of the magi and giving gifts to Jesus on Epiphany would also be a way to enact the story. One might give money to a church or local charity on this special occasion or even give a tangible gift to those in need in the name of Jesus. Serving at a local charity specifically on January 6 could be a way to show Christ's light to the world and to celebrate all God's gifts.

Mardi Gras/Shrove Tuesday

As Epiphany is winding down, it is appropriate to begin preparation for Lenten observance. You may wish to start praying about what disciplines you wish to practice during Lent, so that the turn of the season doesn't catch you unprepared.

In some circles, the day before Ash Wednesday (which begins Lent) is called Shrove Tuesday. The term "shrove" is the past tense of the verb "to shrive," meaning to confess. On this day before Ash Wednesday, Christians approach the season of Lent with confession of sin. Because it is common to fast from rich or fatty foods during Lent, Shrove Tuesday is the last day to employ these ingredients as a way to clean out the pantry for Lent. Churches often host pancake suppers on Shrove Tuesday to symbolize this last rich meal. This consumption of rich foods just before Lent explains the term *Mardi Gras*, French for "Fat Tuesday."

Though the concept of *Mardi Gras* is tied to Lenten observance, today the American celebration of *Mardi Gras* is a thoroughly secular one. The *Carnival* tradition grew up together with Epiphany traditions over time; however, today's *Carnival* season, celebrated with balls, parades, and much merriment, emphasizes feasting without confession or preparation for fasting. The celebration is not moored to the gospel story and is not related to Epiphany.

New Traditions

Perhaps you'd like to send greetings to loved ones during Epiphany instead of during Advent. This is a great way to extend the celebration of Jesus' birth and to share the light of Christ with others, telling them the good news that Jesus is the light of the world. If sending family photos, this timing would allow you to take your photo during Christmastide and then tell others visually and verbally about Christ's light.

One church (in Nashville, TN) gathers to have a bonfire and burn their live Christmas trees on Epiphany to symbolize the light of the world. This might be an event you could do with some friends or neighbors at home, depending on where you live. The light from the fire would be a great conversation starter to share about Jesus and his light. (Do check local ordinances regarding fires.)

Put candles in your windows in order to show forth the light of Christ and as a sign of hospitality to those who pass your home.

Decide to show forth Christ's light in your Twelfth Night party, inviting people from whom you may not get a return invitation. Use this opportunity for hospitality to reach out to different people in your neighborhood or city.

Celebrate the life of Jesus each week in Epiphany by studying gospel narratives. Assign the first week to the adoration of the magi, one to His presentation at the temple, one week to His baptism, one to the miracle at the wedding at Cana. For the remaining weeks choose stories of Jesus healing and teaching during His earthly ministry. Reflect on how Jesus is the light of the world who welcomes Gentiles into the Kingdom of God.

Around the World

Parades: In some countries, such as Poland, Norway, Sweden, Germany, Switzerland, Czech Republic, and Spain, people dress up in costume like the magi and parade through the streets (sometimes even riding on camels).

Gifts: In Italy and some Spanish-speaking countries, children receive presents on Epiphany instead of on Christmas day. In Spanish-speaking countries, children leave their shoes outside and some straw for the camels of the three kings on the evening of January 5, and when they wake their shoes are filled with gifts from the magi instead of from Santa Claus.

Swimming races: In countries where the emphasis of Epiphany is on Jesus' baptism, traditions involving water are primary. In several countries, such as Cyprus and Greece, a small cross is tossed into the water and brave men dive into the frigid waters, racing to catch it. This is an element of a celebration of the blessing of the waters.

Horse races: In Romania, horses blessed with holy water after the blessing of the waters compete in a race.[7]

In the Kitchen

Traditional food for Epiphany centers around the Twelfth Night celebration. Particularly important is the Twelfth Night Cake, also known as King Cake. There are dozens of different recipes for this cake, depending on which region or which country's recipe you bake. In most cases the cake is a spiced one and in many cases, it is formed in the shape of a ring. The most important aspect of this cake is what is hidden inside. Traditionally a bean was hidden inside the cake, but in recent years, some have moved to hide a plastic baby inside the cake. One interesting idea would be to try the recipe from a different country each year.

The drink traditionally served at the Twelfth Night party is a hot spiced drink called Lamb's Wool. Again, recipes abound, both with and without alcohol.

Finally, pancakes are traditionally made on Shrove Tuesday, to use up the sweets and fats in your kitchen before Lent begins.

---

7 These traditions are described in Curtis Wong's *Huffington Post* article and in Tanya Gulevich's *Christmas from A to Z* (Chicago, IL: KWS Publishers, 2011), 138–141.

King Cake Recipe

Dough
- *½ cup (1 stick, 4 ounces) butter, melted*
- *¾ cup (6 ounces) lukewarm milk*
- *2 large eggs + 1 large egg yolk, white reserved*
- *3 ½ cups (14 ¾ ounces) King Arthur Unbleached All-Purpose Flour*
- *¼ cup (1 ¾ ounces) sugar*
- *¼ cup (1 ¼ ounces) Baker's Special Dry Milk or nonfat dried milk powder*
- *1 ¼ teaspoons salt*
- *2 ½ teaspoons instant yeast*
- *¼ teaspoon ground nutmeg*
- *⅛ teaspoon Fiori di Sicilia or lemon oil, or 1 teaspoon grated lemon rind*

Filling
- *8-ounce package cream cheese*
- *½ cup (3 ½ ounces) sugar*
- *3 tablespoons (7/8 ounce) King Arthur Unbleached All-Purpose Flour*
- *1 large egg, lightly beaten*
- *2 teaspoons vanilla or ⅛ teaspoon Fiori di Sicilia or lemon oil*

Icing
- *2 cups (8 ounces) confectioners' sugar*
- *pinch of salt*
- *1 teaspoon vanilla extract*
- *2 tablespoons + 1 to 2 teaspoons milk, enough to make a thick but pourable glaze*

Topping
- *yellow, purple, and green fine sparkling sugars*
- *candied red cherries (optional)*

Method:
1. *Lightly grease a 10", 4-cup capacity bakeable stoneware ring mold, or a baking sheet.*
2. *To prepare the dough: Using a stand mixer, electric hand mixer, or bread machine, mix and knead all of the dough ingredients together to form a smooth, very silky dough. You may try kneading this dough with your hands, if desired; but be advised it's very sticky and soft.*

51

Allow the dough to rise, covered, for 1 hour. It'll become puffy, though it probably won't double in size.

3. *Transfer the soft dough to a lightly greased work surface. Pat and stretch it into a 24" x 6" rectangle. This won't be hard at all; it's very stretchy. Let the dough rest while you prepare the filling.*

4. *To prepare the filling: Beat together the cream cheese, sugar, and flour till smooth, scraping the bowl once. Add the egg and flavor, again beating until smooth.*

5. *Dollop the filling down the center of the long strip of dough. Then fold each edge up and over the filling till they meet at the top; roll and pinch the edges together, to seal the filling inside as much as possible. Don't worry about making the seal look perfect; it'll eventually be hidden by the icing and sugar.*

6. *Place the log of dough into the prepared ring mold, seam down or to the side (just not on top), or onto the baking sheet. The dough will be very extensible, i.e., it'll stretch as you handle it. So pick it up and position it in the pan quickly and gently. Pinch the ends together. Cover and let rise for about an hour, until it's puffy. Preheat the oven to 350°F while the dough rises.*

7. *Whisk the reserved egg white with 1 tablespoon water, and brush it over the risen loaf. Bake the cake for 20 minutes, then tent it lightly with aluminum foil. Bake it for an additional 30 minutes, until it's a rich golden brown. Remove the cake from the oven, and after 5 minutes gently loosen its edges from the pan, if you've baked it in a ring mold. After an additional 10 minutes, turn it out of the pan onto a rack to cool (or transfer it from the baking sheet to a rack to cool).*

8. *To make the icing: Beat together all of the icing ingredients, dribbling in the final 2 teaspoons milk till the icing is thick yet pourable.*

9. *Pour the icing over the completely cooled cake. While it's still sticky, sprinkle with alternating bands of yellow, purple, and green sugars. Space candied cherries in a ring around the top.*

Yield: One loaf, about 16 servings.

This recipe appears courtesy of King Arthur Flour.

For the Very Young

Recruit young helpers to mix up the cake mix and to place the bean or baby into the cake.

Enact the story of the Magi. Let the children dress up as the magi and travel around your yard and house in order to reach Jesus. Talk about the journey and what travel would have been like. When they arrive, have them present their gifts to Jesus.

Let the children decorate the doorstep or sidewalk with chalk as you mark your door frame.

Make the chore of putting away the Christmas decorations into a dance party. Give each child a job to do, so that they can participate, and make sure to sing "We Three Kings" and "What Child is This?" while you work.

Talk about following light in order to see the way. Turn off the lights in your home and let the children use a flashlight to guide them through the house. Then make the connection between the magi following the star, God's word as a light to our path (Psalm 119), and Jesus as the light of the world.

If you are sending out greeting cards, let your children place the stamps on the envelope.

Take turns reciting Epiphany-themed memory verse(s) in the car.

Let the children brainstorm a way to reach out to a neighbor with Christ's love. Give suggestions, but let them make the decision. Then help them carry out their plan.

Things to Make

Crowns: The whole family can wear crowns to enact the story of the magi. If not enacting the story, crowns could serve as a decorative reminder of the story. They could be simple paper crowns or more elaborate ones decorated with jewels.

Candles: Consider making your own candle(s) as a tangible symbol of the light of Christ you desire to show forth as an individual or a family.

Scarves or hats: During the winter season, one way to share the light of Christ may be to help those who may be cold this season. Knitting or crocheting hats or scarves to give away to those in need is a fitting way to celebrate Epiphany.

Beyond the Home

Chalking the doors in your neighborhood is one way to get out of your house and share the good news of Jesus.[8] Consider whether you'd like to meet neighbors that you may not know by offering to chalk their door frames as well.

Serve at a homeless shelter. It is sometimes difficult to find the necessary volunteers to staff the homeless shelter in the weeks surrounding Christmas. Decide to serve as a family or as a group of friends at a shelter. Show forth Christ's light by giving of your time and energy to serve others.

Volunteer at a soup kitchen. Again, think of your service during the cold winter as a way to bring light and warmth into the lives of those suffering.

Pray for your neighbors who do not know Jesus. Pray for opportunities to engage them with the good news of Jesus and also for opportunities to serve them in the coming months.

Consider organizing a monthly neighborhood gathering that would serve to deepen relationships within your community. Building relationships outside your home will give you opportunities to witness to Jesus' light in your life.

Resources

Seasonal Scripture Readings

Matthew 2:1–12: the story of the Magi.
Matthew 3:13–17 (Mark 1:9–11; Luke 3:21–22): baptism of Jesus.
Luke 2:22–40: presentation of Jesus at the temple.
John 2:1–11: the wedding at Cana.

---

8 Lauren Winner discusses this in "20+C+M+B+06: An Epiphany," *Boundless Webzine,* January 6, 2012.

Suggestions for Memorization:

Again Jesus spoke to them, saying, "I am the light of the world. Whoever follows me will not walk in darkness, but will have the light of life." — John 8:12

You are the light of the world. A city set on a hill cannot be hidden. Nor do people light a lamp and put it under a basket, but on a stand, and it gives light to all in the house. In the same way, let your light shine before others, so that they may see your good works and give glory to your Father who is in heaven. — Matthew 5:14–16

Songs of the Season

"What Child Is This?" William Chatterton Dix (1837–1898).
"We Three Kings," John Henry Hopkins, Jr. (1820–1891).
"We Are," Kari Jobe.

Seasonal Reading

"Journey of the Magi" by T.S. Eliot
"For the Time Being: A Christmas Oratorio" by W. H. Auden.

Prayers:

House Blessing: (*You might pray this as you chalk the door frame on January 6)*

> Lord, bless this home and those who live in it. Give them peace, faith, faithfulness, kindness, hospitality, love, and compassion. Give them a sense of your presence here and a desire to show forth your light to others. Bless those who enter and leave this house. In Jesus' name we pray, Amen.

Bedtime Prayer:

O God, by the leading of a star you manifested your only Son to the peoples of the earth; Lead us, who know you now by faith, to your presence, where we may see your glory face to face; through Jesus Christ our Lord, who lives and reigns with you and the Holy Spirit, one God, now and forever. Amen.[9]

---

9 *Book of Common Prayer* (1986), 162.

Lent

by Cate MacDonald

Introduction to Lent

Just as the dark and cold of winter serves to prepare the earth for spring, so the season of Lent reminds us of the more sobering realities of the life of Christ. The Lenten season is made up of 40 days of fasting from certain comforts and conveniences, echoing the time when Christ denied the needs of His own body in preparation for ministry, and fasted for 40 days in the desert.

Traditionally, the Christian church spends the 40 days before Easter — a celebration of the penultimate triumph of Christianity — reminding ourselves that in us the spiritual battle is not yet over. Lent is the longest and most rigorous fast in the church year, and is meant to prepare the church body for the great feast of Easter, through a period of sobriety, generosity, and self-denial.

Lent also echoes the larger truth of the Christian life: that there are times when we will experience hardship and suffering, spiritual winters, and extended darkness. It enlivens us to the harder realities of lifelong faithfulness — that there will be times of absence, doubt, unfulfilled hunger, and unmet spiritual longing — and trains us to follow Christ in times of darkness.

In giving ourselves to a season of less, we learn that our personal comforts have little to do with greater love of Christ. We, like most of God's creatures, are seasonal and should know that some seasons are harsher than others. There are different lessons to be learned, different habits to be employed in winter than in summer. This is as true in our spiritual lives as it is in our gardens or the forest. Lent serves as a time to employ disciplines of self-denial and grow strong in them, rather than weakening ourselves in our constant pursuit of ease and joy. Lent assures us that joy will come later, and it will come surely. Every year our Lenten fasting ends in a resurrection celebration and much feasting, a reminder that hardship will not last for long.

Lent retraces the 40 days of Christ's fast in the desert in which He withstood the temptations of the devil. Matthew, Mark and Luke all tell the story, though Mark's mention is brief. It can be found in Matthew 4:1–11, Luke 4:1–13, and Mark 1:12–13.

Lent is also a time to meditate on Christ's passion and suffering. By denying some of our own desires, we choose to participate in a gentle form of suffering in order to better appreciate Christ's, and to allow ourselves to mourn for His pain and for the sin that caused it. Mourning is a hard thing to do, especially voluntarily, but here too we can be guided by Scripture. Psalm 51 is a beautiful (though challenging) cry for mercy and forgiveness. It is an acknowledgement of sin and of pain, coupled with a request that God would make all things better. It is a wonderful model for Lenten prayer.

The length and customs of Lent vary throughout church traditions and cultures, yet remain united around the shared desire to enter into Christ's suffering, both as He prepared for ministry with a 40-day fast in the desert and as He approached His death on the cross.

It is for this reason that Lent is such a powerful time of year. We are endeavoring, through fasting and much prayer, to emulate a part of Christ's life and nature that is particularly difficult for us, and through the practice of Lent, we confront our sinful tendencies head on, for a long time. To put it simply, Lent is hard and Lent is long, and so Lent is really good for us.

Calendar

In most branches of the western church, Lent starts on Ash Wednesday, which falls 40 days before Easter Sunday, with Sundays excepted and kept as feast days. Though the date of Ash Wednesday is not fixed in the calendar (as it depends on the date of Easter), Lent typically begins in February or March.

Though the entire season of Lent is focused on fasting, there are a few important feast days that usually fall within its boundaries. Chief among them is the annunciation. The annunciation celebrates the visitation of Mary by the angel Gabriel, her obedience to God's will under such an extraordinary request, and the very beginning of Christ's incarnation. It falls on March 25, nine months before Christmas. In the western church, the Feast of the Annunciation is a movable feast, of a sort. If March 25 lands on a Sunday, the feast day is moved to the following Monday; and if March 25 falls within Holy Week, the feast is moved to the Monday following the first Sunday after Easter.

March 19 is Saint Joseph's day, a celebration of Jesus' earthly father. It is a comparatively minor feast day, but seems a fitting day to keep in Lent, given that Joseph was a sacrificial protector and provider for Mary and Jesus, who risked much for the sake of God's Son, with no particular claim to glory or earthly reward for himself.

Saint Patrick's Day is also often celebrated during Lent, as it is kept on March 17. Though Saint Patrick's Day has become an oddly secular pseudo-holiday in the United States, it remains an important feast day, remembering the man who was a great missionary to Ireland and their patron saint.

Traditions

Lenten fasting can and does take many forms. Traditionally, Christians have given up their best food and wine for 40 days, simplifying their meals to better focus their hearts on the life and sacrifice of Christ. It's an excellent idea, but in an age where food preparation takes just a fraction of our time every day, and meals can be wolfed down in front of a television or in the car, many, particularly in Protestantism, choose fasts that will quiet their lives in other ways, whether that be fasting from the television, radio, or social media, or from indulgences of which they are particularly fond, such as sugar or coffee, or from eating at restaurants.

Ephesians 4:22–24 tells us that growing in relationship with and knowledge of Christ is a two-part process that requires the believer "to put off your old self which belongs to your former way of life and is corrupt through deceitful desires" and, instead, to "be renewed in the spirit of your minds, and to put on the new self, created after the likeness of God in true righteousness and holiness." Fasting is, at its core, a discipline of detachment, or a putting off of our old self. By fasting we seek to loosen or break a few of the many holds the world, the flesh, and the devil have in our lives. We detach from food or sweets or television in order to better engage with the Spirit of Christ.

Isaiah 58 offers some keen insights into what a fast should be, and what it should not:

Behold, in the day of your fast you seek your own pleasure,
and oppress all your workers.

> Behold, you fast only to quarrel and to fight
> and to hit with a wicked fist.
> Fasting like yours this day
> will not make your voice to be heard on high.
> Is such the fast that I choose,
> a day for a person to humble himself?
> Is it to bow down his head like a reed,
> and to spread sackcloth and ashes under him?
> Will you call this a fast,
> and a day acceptable to the Lord? (Isa. 58:4–5)

Isaiah (speaking as a prophet in the voice of God) stated that a fast filled with contention and anger, mourning, and false humility is no fast at all. This is interesting given the fact that most would "call this a fast" when we're not eating what we'd like to eat or doing what we'd like to do in order to focus our energy and our bodies on the sustenance the Lord provides. That is the discipline most of us have been taught (if, indeed, we've been taught how to fast at all!); that is the discipline that thousands of Christians are participating in throughout the world during Lent. And yet, no matter how determined or rigorous, it is not enough on its own. Isaiah continues:

> Is not this the fast that I choose:
> to loose the bonds of wickedness,
> to undo the straps of the yoke,
> to let the oppressed go free,
> and to break every yoke?
> Is it not to share your bread with the hungry
> and bring the homeless poor into your house;
> when you see the naked, to cover him,
> and not to hide yourself from your own flesh?
> Then shall your light break forth like the dawn,
> and your healing shall spring up speedily;
> your righteousness shall go before you;
> the glory of the Lord shall be your rear guard.
> Then you shall call, and the Lord will answer;
> you shall cry, and he will say, 'Here I am.' (Isa. 58:6–9)

It appears in this passage that the Lord has chosen a fast that is, in a way, no fast at all. He does not tell us what to give up, but instead what to do. The fast the Lord has chosen is charity, justice, and generosity. The fasting itself is irrelevant — or at least it could be, depending on how you use it. And on closer inspection, it seems all spiritual disciplines are in the same position.

Any discipline that the Lord asks of us is no good by itself. Christians are not like the yogis or the secular ascetics who believe that certain practices by themselves have the power to enlighten. Nor do we believe in a genie of a god who responds best to particular demonstrations of admiration or affection. Any Christian spiritual discipline is undertaken with much prayer and hope. It is a way of quieting the flesh in order to hear God a little more clearly and to speak to Him a little more honestly. His response remains an act of His mercy and goodness, based on nothing but His love. Fasting is an attempt at listening to a Being who can speak very quietly, and there is nothing more noisy than our own wickedness. How will we hear His response to our prayers when our own voice uses the fast that was meant to quiet it as a loudspeaker, happily abusing the downtrodden or making a show of our self-denial for the benefit of those more easily fooled than the Almighty? It will be of no benefit to us, and might do damage.

With this in mind, it's important to consider what you might choose to take on during your Lenten fast. Fasting is a discipline of denial which depends on what you put in the place of that from which you as fasting. Traditionally, fasting Christians have used their meal times to pray, and their hunger pangs as reminders to seek the Lord in prayer. Scripture memorization is also an excellent, time-honored choice, as are special acts of charity and almsgiving. Scripture is quite clear that fasting is only as good as the spirit with which it is undertaken. And so one takes up a new discipline in the place of the comfort that is being put off: charity for indulgence, or prayer for food. This is especially important to keep in mind during Lent, when the timing and duration of the fast has been chosen for you. It would be easy to fall into the temptation of merely doing what is required of you, such as fasting from meat or wine, without considering what you should do instead to best use your time of fasting.

In *Sermons on the Statutes*, Saint John Chrysostom reiterates this point saying:

Do you fast? Give me proof of it by your works.
If you see a poor man, take pity on him.
If you see a friend being honored, do not envy him.

Do not let only your mouth fast, but also the eye and the ear and the feet
and the hands and all the members of our bodies.
Let the hands fast, by being free of avarice.
Let the feet fast, by ceasing to run after sin.
Let the eyes fast, by disciplining them not to glare at that which is sinful.
Let the ear fast, by not listening to evil talk and gossip.
Let the mouth fast from foul words and unjust criticism.
For what good is it if we abstain from birds and fishes, but bite and devour our brothers?
May He who came to the world to save sinners strengthen us to complete the fast with humility, have mercy on us and save us.[1]

Like Isaiah, Chrysostom was interested primarily in how we act when we fast, not the particulars of what we are ostensibly fasting from. Jesus too offered instructions for fasting in Matthew 6:16–18, but they were also focused on one's public appearance and behavior rather than the method or means of a private fast. He didn't seem particularly concerned with what one fasted from, but asked that a fast be kept in the quiet of one's home, and that those who fast behave as well or better than when they're not fasting. Though Lent enforces a kind of public fast since we are participating in it together, your particular discipline, choices, or rhythms should never be used to make others notice your own devotion to Christ or to the season, but be kept quietly, even when kept corporately.

The corporate nature of Lent can be of particular help to those new to fasting. When undertaken well you will have a parish supporting you, and at least weekly reminders to stay dedicated to your discipline. Lent can serve as a training ground for how to undertake private fasting in the future. Seek out the mature and the wise in your parish and learn from them during the season of fasting that you undertake together.

Despite differences in what we chose to fast from, all Christian should use the season of Lent to better love and serve our neighbors and our families, to champion the oppressed, and lift up the downtrod-

---

1 This translation of John Chrysostom's sermon, widely available online, is not attributed. Our gratitude is extended to the translator, whose work has benefited us and others.

den. To be truly, in a word, Christians.

New Traditions

The first question for most Protestants approaching Lent is what to fast from. One may choose to take on a traditional fast from meat and alcohol (or from all meat, dairy, alcohol and olive oil, if you want to follow the eastern tradition), but many will find that, particularly in family life, there are other fasts that will have a greater impact.

Fasts from objects other than food can be particularly helpful to children, especially if they choose them themselves. After all, their food is made and often decided for them by their parents anyway, and their parents will need decide on and prepare for any food fast as well, but fasts from other things such as television can be undertaken by the child herself and may be of greater benefit (more about this in the *For the Very Young* section).

Turning off some of the noise that surrounds modern life is a particularly good fast for many families or for very busy people, whether that is the television, the car stereo, the internet, or too many after-school activities. T.S. Eliot's famous work "Ash Wednesday" contains a haunting phrase, "Where shall the word be found, where will the word/ Resound? Not here, there is not enough silence." It's a good reminder that in order to hear from God, we may be required to calm the many noises in our own life. Sit down with your family, or in the quiet of your own heart, and decide how you might put off some of the noise in your house through fasting so that you can learn to hear the resounding Word of God.

Spring-cleaning has become something of a Lenten sub-tradition, as Lent often coincides with the coming of spring, and fasting has a way of digging into other areas of one's life. Lenten discipline may well encourage you to clean some of the clutter and dirt out of your home as you do the same to your soul. Similarly, many mainline churches keep a tradition of the Altar Guild thoroughly cleaning the church at the end of Lent, in preparation for Easter.

George Herbert's feast day is February 27, and so it either falls within the boundaries of Lent or quite near to it. It's a minor occasion in comparison with the many feast days of the great and more famous saints the church recognizes throughout the year, but the poetry of Herbert is lovely and approachable, even for the young. It would be a good time to read and perhaps begin to memorize his beautiful poem

"Lent," taking particular notice that he begins by calling it a feast. See *Resources* section at the end of this chapter for the complete text of the poem.

T.S. Eliot's "Ash Wednesday" is a more complex and subtle meditation on Lent, but no less beautiful. You might take time to read it with friends or older children and meditate on his reflections on noise and mortality.

As was mentioned in the *Calendar* section, St. Patrick's Day often falls within the boundaries of Lent. Any of the traditional celebrations related to St. Patrick's can be fun for children, but in keeping with the spirit of Lent, it would be important to meditate on and share with your family who St. Patrick really was and what he did. It's also an ideal time to memorize a portion of "St. Patrick's Breastplate." See *Resources* section for the text of this poem.

Around the World

Many of Lent's most important traditions, such as fasting and acts of service, are observed throughout most Christian traditions around the world. Though calendar and liturgy may vary, the spirit of the season remains consistent.

Shrove Tuesday and the days immediately before Lent have taken on the marks of various cultures — from the Brazilian or Venetian Carnival and Louisiana's *Mardi Gras,* to family-oriented pancake dinners at churches throughout the United States.

Fasting traditions vary depending on one's church tradition, which naturally creates differences throughout cultures as well. In the western world, abstinence from meat on Fridays results in the strange phenomenon of limited-time only fast food fish sandwiches, while more traditional, Eastern Orthodox cultures abstain from meat altogether.

Ultimately, the consistencies of the Lenten season throughout the world are more prominent than the differences, reflecting the seemingly simple truth that no matter where we live, the season of remembrance is much needed.

In the Kitchen

The Lenten kitchen will depend on how you keep your Lent. You may decide to keep a vegetarian fast throughout the week, or just on Fridays in keeping with various traditions. You might also want to find recipes that help you simplify your life, and allow you time and space to keep your fast. Crock-Pot bean chilies or vegetable soups will help you achieve both goals.

If simplifying your meals and limiting your time in the kitchen would best serve your fast, then there are many websites and resources for once a month or once a week cooking, which requires a great effort one or two days a month or week and then allows the cook more time throughout the rest of the week.

St. Patrick's Day is a wonderful time to try some new, traditionally Irish foods, including soda bread, corned beef, shepherd's pie, and potato candy (really! Potato candy!).

Sundays in Lent are traditionally feast days, a weekly reminder that the resurrection has come and is coming again. If you don't keep a weekly Sunday dinner as a family or with members of your parish, Lent could be a wonderful time to start. Make your Sunday a special day of worship, feasting, rest, and fellowship during this rigorous time of the church year.

For the Very Young

Lent is not a particularly fun time in the church year, and its significance is complex. Take care to help young children understand Lent as well as they can, in a way that requires some volition on their part. Even a two-year-old knows that she is supposed to share her toys, and it might be possible that by three she could understand enough about Jesus to want to do something for Him. Lent is the perfect time to allow her to try.

Allow young children to choose a fast for themselves, if they are able. Perhaps there is a toy or TV show or game they would be willing to give up for the season. Encourage them to consider what they might do instead, such as visiting Grandma, helping clean the church or house, memorizing a short passage of Scripture or a poem, or acts of special kindness towards their siblings. In this way you are encouraging them to understand the dual nature of fasting: that "putting off" is only good when we take on something better.

As Lent begins, take some time to talk about Jesus' fast in the wilderness, and what it means to be tempted. Allow them to reflect on what they're tempted towards (anger towards their sister, selfishness with their toys, not wanting to do their school work), and assist them in seeing that Jesus too was tempted, and knows how it feels and how hard it can be to resist, but that His steadfastness in the face of such temptation is part of what we're remembering in these 40 days.

Incorporate a daily devotional time for the whole family. It might be a good time for parents to read one of the Gospels to children, maybe from a children's Bible, so even the little children could have Jesus' life and ministry in mind by the time we enter Holy Week and reflect on His passion.

The stations of the cross, as pictorial representations of the passion of Christ broken into stages, are a good tool for teaching children about Holy Week as Lent comes to an end. Find a local church with the stations and open visiting hours so that you can walk your children through them at their own pace and talk about each stage. For the very young, you may need to take a couple trips to get through them.[2]

As has been mentioned in previous sections, fasting from food is often not the most meaningful fast that can be taken by children, and it should also be noted that it might not be safe for them. The very young should never be required to restrict their food intake, nor should growing children, nor pregnant or nursing mothers. Those in a weakened state of health would be wise to consult their doctor, or choose another fast.

Things to Make

Reflections journal: Lent is a time of sobriety and reflection, and a journal, perhaps kept over several years of Lent and set aside between, is a good way of recording your journey through the season. Even children could keep a journal, just a sentence every couple of days for the young, written by their parent if they can't yet write, and a bit longer for older members of the household, reflecting on the effects of their fast in both themselves and their home.

If you're keeping a food fast (such as deciding to go meatless) then you will most likely be eating new things, and trying new recipes. Include your family and friends in some of them and make "fast food" together.

Creating handcrafts that are meant to be given away is particularly appropriate for the season. There are many charities around the world that need receiving blankets for new mothers, or teddy bears for

---

2 For those concerned about violations of the second commandment, the stations of the cross can be observed without pictorial representation of Christ Himself, but with only the events of His passion.

children in disaster zones. If you're skipping a meal during any part of your Lent, making something for someone else might be a good way to spend the time you would have otherwise spent eating.

Charity is an important part of Lent, and you may decide to create gift baskets for those in need within your community. They might be for an elderly friend or relative in a convalescent home, or supply boxes for the homeless or needy. Spend time you might have otherwise spent on relaxing or entertaining yourself creating something for someone else.

Beyond the Home

Practices of charity and alms giving are traditional and essential parts of Lent. In keeping with Isaiah 58, Lent should be a time of great hospitality, kindness, and generosity.

Reach out to the needy and the vulnerable such as orphans, widows, the homeless, and the oppressed.

If you're fasting from shopping or something of the like, consider donating the money saved to a trustworthy charity devoted to serving hungry or orphaned children in dangerous parts of the world.

If you've fasted from an activity or entertainment choice and so have extra time, you can spend some of it caring for the lonely, such as the elderly in your neighborhood who are far from family.

If you know any new mothers, cook for them and clean their homes, if they'll let you. They're worn out, and laborious housework is good for your soul.

Find out what your church needs as it approaches Easter. If you're at a sacramental church, your altar may be bare for the first time in a year, and there may be special work to do before it's ready to be restored.

Pray often and fervently. Pray for your community, your church, your family, and your home.

After having provided all these suggestions on things to do during Lent, let me provide the caveat that it would be a great disservice to yourself and your faith to busy yourself during a time of fasting in order to ignore or ride over the feelings it might bring up. Fasting for 40 days is difficult (it was even for Jesus), and part of the reason we fast is because it is difficult. Fasting is a time to mourn for one's sin and the pain that it caused our beloved Savior. Though part of the way you may participate in mourning is by serving those who have been particularly affected by the results of living in a fallen world (such as those named above), it may be that God is asking you to be quiet, to spend real time with Him and the depths of your own soul. This is where the prayer of *Examen* (see *Resources* section) will be of help to you. Keep watch on your motivations and your heart, whatever fast you choose, in order to keep a true and holy Lent.

Resources

Seasonal Scripture Readings

The Book of Lamentations
Exodus 16–17
Isaiah 53 and 58
Psalm 51
Psalms 4, 6, 17, 22, 25, 32, 41, 42, 73, 102, 121, and 130
Luke 4:1–13

Suggestions for Memorization:

For I was hungry and you gave me food, I was thirsty and you gave me drink, I was a stranger and you welcomed me, I was naked and you clothed me, I was sick and you visited me, I was in prison and you came to me. Then the righteous will answer him, saying, "Lord, when did we see you hungry and feed you, or thirsty and give you drink? And when did we see you a stranger and welcome you, or naked and clothe you? And when did we see you sick or in prison and visit you?" And the King will answer them, "Truly I say to you as you did it to one of the least of these, my brothers, you did it to me." — Matthew 25:35–40

Have this mind among yourselves, which is yours in Christ Jesus, who, though he was in the form of God, did not count equality with God a thing to be grasped, but made himself nothing, taking the form of a servant, being born in the likeness of men. And being found in human form, he humbled himself by

becoming obedient to the point of death, even death on the cross.
— Philippians 2:5–9

Is not this the fast that I choose: to loose the bonds of wickedness,
to undo the straps of the yoke, to let the oppressed go free, and to
break every yoke? Is it not to share your bread with the hungry
and bring the homeless poor into your house; when you see the
naked to cover him and not to hide yourself from your own flesh?
Then shall your light break forth like the dawn, and your
healing shall spring up speedily; your righteousness shall go up
before you; the glory of the Lord shall be your rear guard. — Isa-
iah 58:6–8

Songs of the Season

Lent is a season of remembrance and solemnity, and the songs of the
season reflect both, some with profound beauty.

St. Matthew's Passion: One of Johann Sebastian Bach's great sacred
masterworks, *St. Matthew's Passion* tells the story of Christ's death, as
told through the gospel of Matthew and a series of choruses from
those who demand the crucifixion. When listening you may encounter
a familiar melody, one that has become best known as "O Sacred Head
Sore Wounded,"[3] a hymn reflecting on our role in Christ's death and
the immensity of his sacrifice.

Sung in German, it is well worth reading the English libretto as a
devotional guide while you listen.

John Ritter's *Requiem*: *Requiem* is another great sacred work focused on the passion of Christ and the nature of death. Sung in a
series of choruses and solos, it is a solemn, but ultimately triumphant,
reflection on the season.

Benjamin Britten's *Abraham and Isaac* is a haunting meditation on
sacrifice and the will of God.

Hymns of the Season:

"O Sacred Head Sore Wounded"
"Love Divine, All Loves Excelling"

---

3 In some hymnals and traditions, this hymn is entitled, "O Sacred Head, Now
Wounded."

"Kyrie Eleison"
"What a Friend We Have in Jesus"
"O Love that Will Not Let Me Go"
"Just As I Am"
"Jesus, Remember Me"

Seasonal Reading

Spiritual Disciplines Handbook, by Adele Calhoun: The handbook is a wonderful resource of spiritual disciplines with detailed descriptions of why they are undertaken, how to do them well, and their scriptural foundations. She has special chapters on fasting and types of prayer that will be useful to keeping a good Lent.

The Divine Hours: Prayers for Spring Time, by Phyllis Tickle: *The Divine Hours* can be used throughout the year to follow a rhythm of prayer and Scripture reading two to three times a day. Following the hours is an excellent Lenten discipline.

Book of Common Prayer: The Anglican guide to prayer and worship. An invaluable resource throughout the church year.

Celtic Daily Prayer: A prayer manual from the Northumbria community, containing daily prayer guides, and the prayers of St. Patrick, among others.

T.S. Eliot's poem "Ash Wednesday"

George Herbert's "Lent":

> Welcome dear feast of Lent: who loves not thee,
> He loves not Temperance, or Authority,
> But is compos'd of passion.
> The Scriptures bid us fast; the Church says, now:
> Give to thy Mother, what thou wouldst allow
> To ev'ry Corporation.
>
> The humble soul compos'd of love and fear
> Begins at home, and lays the burden there,
> When doctrines disagree,
> He says, in things which use hath justly got,
> I am a scandal to the Church, and not
> The Church is so to me.
>
> True Christians should be glad of an occasion
> To use their temperance, seeking no evasion,
> When good is seasonable;

Unless Authority, which should increase
The obligation in us, make it less,
And Power itself disable.

Besides the cleanness of sweet abstinence,
Quick thoughts and motions at a small expense,
A face not fearing light.
Whereas in fulness there are sluttish fumes,
Sour exhalations, and dishonest rheums,
Revenging the delight.

Then those same pendant profits, which the spring
And Easter intimate, enlarge the thing,
And goodness of the deed.
Neither ought other men's abuse of Lent
Spoil the good use; lest by that argument
We forfeit all our Creed.

It's true, we cannot reach Christ's forti'eth day;
Yet to go part of that religious way,
Is better than to rest:
We cannot reach our Saviour's purity;
Yet we are bid, 'Be holy ev'n as he,'
In both let's do our best.

Who goeth in the way which Christ hath gone,
Is much more sure to meet with him, than one
That travelleth by-ways:
Perhaps my God, though he be far before,
May turn and take me by the hand, and more:
May strengthen my decays.

Yet Lord instruct us to improve our fast
By starving sin and taking such repast,
As may our faults control:
That ev'ry man may revel at his door,
Not in his parlour; banqueting the poor,
And among those his soul.

"St. Patrick's Breastplate":

Christ be with me, Christ within me,
Christ behind me, Christ before me,

Christ beside me, Christ to win me,
Christ to comfort and restore me.
Christ beneath me, Christ above me,
Christ in quiet, Christ in danger,
Christ in hearts of all that love me,
Christ in mouth of friend and stranger.[4]

St. Patrick's Day and Lent

When St. Patrick's Day falls within Lent, there are many craft-
ing and creating opportunities, whether that be paper shamrocks
or Irish soda bread. St. Patrick's Day is pretty goofy in the United
States at large, but that doesn't mean it can't be meaningful. Re-
member Saint Patrick as the "converter of Ireland," and a great
missionary and bishop. If you have young children, you could en-
joy reenacting some of his more mythical activities, such as chas-
ing all the snakes from Ireland into the sea, never to return. Plen-
ty of little boys with toy snakes would be happy to dump them into
their kiddie pool or a nearby stream in the spirit of St. Patrick.

Prayers

Fasting is at the service of prayer, and is made less than useless without
it. So in addition to particular prayers included here, keep in mind that
frequent prayer, whatever the subject needs to be, is the heart and soul
of Lent.

Traditionally, Lent, as a preparation for Christ's passion, is held as
a time to contemplate one's mortality. In many churches, Lent starts
with the Ash Wednesday service, for which the priest will have burnt
the ashes of palms used on the previous Palm Sunday and used the
ashes to make the sign of the cross on his parishioners' foreheads. *The*
Book of Common Prayer's Ash Wednesday service, which is used in the
service before the ashes are distributed, includes a beautiful invitation

---

4 The portion of the Breastplate provided here is just a small selection of the much
longer hymn.

to Lent that can be used as a daily reminder of what you are participating in:

> I invite you, therefore, in the name of the Church, to the ob-
> servance of a holy Lent, by self-examination and repentance;
> by prayer, fasting, and self-denial; and by reading and medi-
> tating on God's holy Word.

> To make a right beginning of repentance, and as a mark of
> our mortal nature, let us now kneel before the Lord, our mak-
> er and redeemer.

> ...Grant that these ashes may be a sign of our mortality and
> penitence, that we may remember that it is only by your gra-
> cious gift that we are given everlasting life, through Jesus
> Christ our Savior.

> ...Remember that you are dust, and to dust you shall return.[5]

In this invitation is the exhortation to remain consistently in
God's word, to pray, and to remember your own sin and mortality. It is
a concise reminder of the essence of the season.

In *A Manual of Eastern Orthodox Prayers*, there is a beautiful prayer
written by Philaret, Metropolitan of Moscow, that, though not strictly
for Lent, can be made of good use, especially to combat the irritability
that can come from fasting:

> O Lord, grant me to greet the coming day in peace. Help
> me in all things to rely upon Your holy will. In every hour
> of the day reveal Your will to me. Bless my dealings with all
> who surround me. Teach me to treat all that comes to me
> throughout the day with peace of soul, and with firm con-
> viction that Your will governs all. In all my deeds and words
> guide my thoughts and feelings. In unforeseen events let me
> not forget that all are sent by You. Teach me to act firmly and
> wisely, without embittering and embarrassing others. Give
> me strength to bear the fatigue of the coming day with all
> that it shall bring. Direct my will, teach me to pray, pray You
> Yourself in me. Amen.

The Ignatian prayer of *Examen* is particularly fitting during the
season of Lent, as it may help you identify whether you are keeping the

---

5 *Book of Common Prayer* (1986), 265.

true fast spoken of in Isaiah 58, and where you could do better as you continue on through the season. Ignatius of Loyola discusses the use of the *Examen* in his *Spiritual Exercises*, the basic format of which is to take at least a few minutes at the end of your day to do the following:

Become aware of God's presence where you are.
Review the day with thankfulness and gratitude.
Acknowledge any emotions that were present throughout the day or now.
Choose one feature of the day and pray from it or for it.
Look toward tomorrow, pray that God be with you.

Holy Week

by Jennifer Snell

Introduction to Holy Week

In the Christian calendar, our year-long celebration of God's grace, Holy Week marks the end of Jesus' earthly life. His suffering, death, and resurrection form the crux of our faith and the reason for our hope. This is the drama the whole church year hinges on, and the traditions of Holy Week invite us to contemplate, follow, and enter into the events of Jesus' life the week He died.

Holy Week begins on the Sunday before Easter, Palm Sunday, which is the commemoration of Jesus' climactic entry in Jerusalem before the Passover festival. The royal homage Jesus received along the way started the week with a triumphal tone, but events soon turned to scandal as Jesus' messianic actions set in motion the events that culminated in His execution.

The finale of Holy Week is the three days known as the *Triduum*[1]: Maundy Thursday, Good Friday, and Holy Saturday. During these long days of Holy Week we face the hard, startling reality of Jesus' last supper with His disciples, His agony in the garden, His scourging, crowning with thorns, carrying of the cross, crucifixion, death, and burial. The Triduum presents the extent of Jesus' passion and presses upon us the truth of Jesus' death as a real event.

And it was an event that left His disciples bereft and confused. Not until after Jesus' resurrection did the meaning of His passion become clear to them. The two travelers on the road to Emmaus lamented, "We had hoped that he was the one to redeem Israel" (Luke 24:21), but they couldn't recognize the redemption. So Jesus Himself explained the mystery to them, saying, "'O foolish ones, and slow of heart to believe all that the prophets have spoken! Was it not necessary that the Christ should suffer these things and enter into his glory?' And begin-

---

1 Pronounced "tri-juh-wuhm" (*tri-jə-wəm*).

ning with Moses and all the Prophets, he interpreted to them in all the Scriptures the things concerning himself" (24:25–27).

Jesus unlocked the Scriptures and the Scriptures unlocked the meaning of the drama. Popular imagination had seized upon the idea of a conquering hero, but Scripture foretold a suffering servant, a humble king. In the light of Scripture, the Messiah who would give His life was not an absurd contradiction but the very fulfillment of God's promise to redeem the world. While walking and then breaking bread with the risen Jesus, the disciples realized that the promises had become reality.

As Christians, we experience the events of Holy Week in the context of this miraculous ending: God raised Jesus from the dead and made Him both Lord and Messiah (Acts 2:24, 36). The Son of God came and accomplished the ultimate Passover — overcoming the grave and passing from death to life. All our worship is undergirded by the events of the *Triduum*, of Jesus' last supper with His disciples, His passion and crucifixion, and His rising to new life. Nevertheless, during the Holy Week anniversary of these events, we dwell on them with devoted attention so that their meaning renews our mindset for our day-to-day sacrifices.

To celebrate Holy Week is to seek the face of God. In Jesus, the eternal Son of God has a human face. But there's more. Even better than knowing that the Messiah has come is glimpsing the fullness of divine love He personifies. This glimpse is the meaning of the Holy Week traditions. The memorials derive from the same elements that inspired the disciples; we walk with Jesus through Scripture and encounter Him in the breaking of bread.

Infused with Scripture, the traditions illumine the endless profundity of Christ's passion as a total gift of love: "Christ... loved me and gave himself for me" (Gal. 2:20). Engaging year after year with the representations of humility in the Holy Week celebrations uncovers layers of significance and relevance: "[Christ] disarmed the powers and authorities... triumphing over them by the cross" (Col. 2:15, NIV) and, "In Christ God was reconciling the world to himself" (II Cor. 5:19). The traditions reveal the dimensions of God's inexhaustible love, a love that is meant to be celebrated and shared in the world, in the church, in the home.

And in our lives. Holy Week is not a thought project but an immersion experience. Jesus went through hell and back so our lives could become immersed in God's life — in true, thorough, selfless, generous, life-giving love. We try to come to grips with this truth, but instead it grips us. The beauty of Holy Week is that "we all, with unveiled face, beholding the glory of the Lord, are being transformed into the same image from one degree of glory to another" (II Cor. 3:18). We celebrate to behold; we behold to be transformed. Our Holy Week worship doesn't make Christ's death any less shocking, but the shock turns out to be that God's glory and victory and love are more amazing than we ever imagined.

Calendar

The timing of Holy Week depends on Easter (see the next chapter, *Easter*, for an explanation of the dating of Easter). During the earliest centuries of Christendom, Christians celebrated Christ's death and resurrection in one all-night vigil between the Saturday and Sunday of Easter. In preparation for the vigil, fasting began on Friday, extending the festival over three days.

After the edict of toleration by Constantine (AD 313), Christians began commemorating other events from the week of Christ's passion: the procession of palms on Sunday, the Last Supper on Holy Thursday, and the cross on Good Friday. Holy Week as we know it today still follows that same structure from the fourth century: Palm Sunday, Holy Thursday, Good Friday, and Holy Saturday. (The Easter Vigil traditions are covered in the next chapter.)

Today Holy Thursday is also called Maundy Thursday and is considered in the Western churches to be the end of Lent and the beginning of the *Triduum*. Although Palm Sunday and each day of the *Triduum* have a distinct emphasis, Holy Week is a continuum, and the one underlying theme is God's salvation in Christ "in whom we have redemption, the forgiveness of sins" (Col. 1:14).

Traditions

Like so many of the traditions of the church year, the Holy Week traditions are steeped in Scripture. Essentially, the traditions are Scripture read aloud, prayed aloud, and imitated communally. This corporate engagement with Scripture was especially necessary during the many centuries when public readings were the standard option for learning Scripture, before the invention of the printing press and the widespread distribution of Bibles. What Scripture reveals, the traditions impart to the community. And the revelation of Scripture is nothing less than the life of God Himself, made available to us: "These are written so that you may believe that Jesus is the Christ, the Son of God, and that by believing you may have life in his name" (John 20:31). Encountering God and His life-giving power: this is why the Scriptures were written and why they undergird our Holy Week celebrations.

In addition to the words and events of Scripture, the Holy Week traditions focus also on the places in Scripture where Christ journeyed. Holy Week draws attention and pilgrims to those locations so that where Christ has gone, we may be found as well. Theologian Fred Sanders explains how we share in Christ's own journey: "God the Holy Spirit places us into what God the Father has done in Christ so that we go to the cross and come out of the tomb in him. Galilee, Gethsemane, and Calvary are not just distant events in the prior biography of our present Savior. Christ is present to us through the Spirit, in the power of that finished work, and our salvation has the shape of dying and rising with him."[2] Once we recognize the goal: union with God in Christ through the Spirit, we can begin to appreciate the Holy Week traditions that point us to that destination.

Palm Sunday

The bookends to Holy Week are Palm Sunday and Easter. Holy Week dawns with Palm Sunday, the last Sunday in Lent, and then culminates a week later in Easter Sunday. Palm Sunday sets the stage for Holy Week and anticipates the even more glorious celebration of Easter at the conclusion of Holy Week. Palm Sunday takes its name from Jesus' triumphal entry into Jerusalem, when the disciples and crowds waved palms to cheer their Messiah on toward victory. The ancient tradition for Palm Sunday invites us to celebrate this occasion by imitating it. All over the world, Palm Sunday finds Christians raising palms or other branches, marching around their neighborhoods and churches, chanting the same royal psalms, honoring Christ as Redeemer and King. Palm Sunday is not a spectator sport but a victory march in which we are the participants.

Once the procession reaches the church, the Scripture lessons for Palm Sunday continue the saga of what happened to Christ after He entered Jerusalem. There He suffered and died. The Gospel writers recorded more details about this period than any other in Jesus' life. Their narratives

---

2 Fred Sanders, *The Deep Things of God* (Wheaton, IL: Crossway Books, 2010), 174.

contain many allusions to Old Testament prophecies in order to indicate the significance of the events. Therefore the Gospel lessons read aloud for Palm Sunday have intricate depth and breadth. The readings are called Passion Gospels in reference to the passion, the suffering, of Christ; the emphasis on the long Passion Gospel (either from Matthew, Mark, or Luke) gives Palm Sunday its full title of the Sunday of the Passion. Often congregations will assign different readers to portray specific roles, so the dramatic presentation of the Passion Gospel involves everyone present. Once again, the Palm Sunday traditions beg us to become invested. With this introduction to Holy Week, we do not sidestep the real cost of Christ's victory over death: His own suffering and death.

Maundy Thursday

The evening of the Thursday in Holy Week is now considered to be the start of the Easter *Triduum*, the sacred three days which form the core of the church year. The ancient name for this day, the "Thursday of the Lord's Supper," indicates the main event commemorated: Jesus' Last Supper with His disciples the night before He died. The context of Holy Week highlights the Lord's Supper as a memorial of Christ's sacrificial death. "For whenever you eat this bread and drink this cup, you proclaim the Lord's death until he comes" (I Cor. 11:26). During the rest of the church year, every celebration of the Lord's Supper connects to Christ's complete offering of Himself for our vivification — the focus of Holy Week.

The gospel of John also relates how Jesus washed the feet of His disciples before His death, giving them a concrete example of humble love. Jesus explained His service as "A new commandment I give to you, that you love one another: just as I have loved you, you also are to love one another" (John 13:34). The Latin word *mandatum* for "command" gives Holy Thursday its common name of Maundy Thursday. The traditional observance for this day has long included foot-washing; for example, abbots and kings used to wash the feet of commoners on this day. Today many churches hold a moving foot-washing ceremony on Maundy Thursday, startling participants out of their comfort zones as they kneel to handle one another's dirty feet.

Maundy Thursday concludes with a nocturnal prayer vigil, a tradition to honor Christ's last sleepless night of agony in the Garden of Gethsemane. Jesus asked His disciples to keep watch with Him, but they slept instead. Therefore, the Maundy Thursday Watch invites us to take Christ's request personally, that through prayer we may be in His company.

Good Friday

In the chronology of Holy Week, Good Friday aligns with the day Christ died. The oldest tradition for this day is to mark it by fasting. The name "Good Friday" invites the question, why is it called Good? The ancient meaning of "Good" is "Holy," which is the fitting description for the day that Christ's sacrifice won our salvation. In the gospels, the Friday of Christ's death coincided with the day of the Passover sacrifice. At the same hour when the Passover lambs were sacrificed in the temple, Jesus cried, "It is finished," and breathed His last (John 19:30). Jesus' death in connection to Passover clarified the meaning of His death as sacrifice, the supreme sacrifice of the perfect Passover Lamb of God (I Cor. 5:7). The traditional Scripture readings for Good Friday bring out this theme. The Passion gospel featured on Good Friday has typically been the gospel of John. More than the other Passion narratives, John's majestic writing highlights the victory of Christ's death on the cross; it was the hour "for the Son of Man to be glorified" (John 12:23). Though Good Friday warrants fasting and mourning, the bedrock ever remains the extent of God's love "in that while we were still sinners, Christ died for us" (Rom. 5:8).

Good Friday is also the one day of the church year which has preserved some of the most ancient elements from Christian worship. Lengthy prayers on behalf of humanity were commonplace in the early church; now Good Friday continues the tradition of these solemn intercessions for the whole world. There is also a long history of devotions inspired by Good Friday's themes: the cross of Christ, Christ's painful walk to Calvary or "The Way of the Cross", his "Three Hours" in crucified agony, the "Seven Last Words" of Christ uttered before death, and more. Countless past and present artists have created beautiful accompaniments for these devotions. With the treasure trove of hymns, poems, art, and music associated with Good Friday, we have abundant inspiration for our ongoing remembrance of Christ's redemptive passion.

Holy Saturday

After sunset on Holy Saturday, the great vigil of Easter begins. In the story of the church year, the Easter vigil is the first and foremost feast (but that's a subject for the next chapter). The tradition for the day of Holy Saturday continues to be fasting and preparing for the vigil. One common prayer for the day encapsulates the theme of waiting for the resurrection: "O God, Creator of heaven and earth: Grant that, as the crucified body of your dear Son was laid in the tomb and rested on this holy Sabbath, so we may await with him the coming of the third day, and rise with him to newness of life...."[3]

But the earliest Christian images of Christ's death and resurrection communicate what Christ did behind-the-scenes this Sabbath day. Not only did He descend to the dead; He released the captives there: "For Christ also suffered once for sins, the righteous for the unrighteous, that he might bring us to God, being put to death in the flesh but made alive in the spirit, in which he went and proclaimed to the spirits in prison, because they formerly did not obey, when God's patience waited in the days of Noah, while the ark was being prepared, in which a few, that is, eight persons, were brought safely through water" (I Pet. 3:18–20). Christ's "Harrowing of Hell," with its long tradition in art and music, signifies Holy Saturday not as a day of quiet resting but a day of decisive triumph over hell and death.

New Traditions

Show up. See for yourself the relevance of your local *Triduum* and Sunday services. No private devotion can substitute for the corporate journey to Easter in the company of your church. As we have seen, the ancient Holy Week customs involve much creativity and drama, and they happen only once a year. The artful traditions tell the gospel story in words, gestures, symbols, and music, involving our bodies and imaginations. To celebrate Christ's victory is what it means to be Christian, and these celebrations are meant to bring unity to the body of Christ.

Clear your calendar. When a friend or family member dies, our daily routine halts. The immediate concern becomes the memorial service and the funeral preparations. We do not expect ourselves to carry on with other events and activities. For Christians, this time of year demands our pause. By slowing down and clearing away our other time-consuming distractions, we are more prepared to savor the meaning of these celebrations. Especially for Good Friday, ask for time off from work or school. Disengage from media consumption during the time from Holy Thursday to Easter Sunday. Meeting Christ in the

---

3 Collect for Holy Saturday, *Book of Common Prayer (1986)*.

Triduum celebrations deserves our priority.

See Jerusalem. Even if your visit does not coincide with Holy Week, take your once-in-a-lifetime pilgrimage to the Holy Land. The places where Jesus acted are still there, and you can experience them. Through walking where He walked, the gospel becomes more than words on a page. We can then envision the Holy Week events with vivid clarity, as we see their original setting and location.

Make a pilgrimage. If you cannot travel all the way to Jerusalem for your Easter break, celebrate the *Triduum* at another destination. Various retreat houses, churches, and seminaries offer Holy Week retreats so you can celebrate this climax of the church year with their community. These groups welcome your presence and participation, so don't feel left out if your local church does not have *Triduum* services. Getting away also removes the preoccupations that compete for our attention, allowing us to participate fully in the celebrations.

Celebrate with others. If you miss an occasion at church, bring it home. The wealth of Holy Week is overwhelming, and few people have the luxury of attending every possible service. Take in what you can, without treating Holy Week like a checklist. Then pick the traditions you might share with others in a home setting, such as foot-washing, keeping vigil, or reading the passion gospels.

Find an old tradition that is new to you. For example, discover the Passover backdrop to the *Triduum* by attending a Passover Seder at your local Messianic congregation or with your Jewish friends. Respecting that this Jewish ritual is not a do-it-yourself affair, we can join with others who celebrate this sacred meal to honor God's Passover deliverance of His people.

Enjoy the smorgasbord. Holy Week has inspired countless works of art, music, poetry, film, and more. The *Resources* section of this chapter contains references to these creations that capture our imagination and aid our meditation. Pick what interests you, whether to watch, hear, read, hold, or taste. Hopefully some of these ideas will become your new favorite family traditions for Holy Week.

Around the World

Congregations all over the world have developed their own artwork and devotions for a famous Holy Week tradition: the Stations of the Cross. Individual churches display representations of the passion scenes at "stations" around the church walls or gardens. The prayer walk from station to station, like a pilgrimage to the holy sites, invites participants to recognize the journey of Christ on the road to Calvary, and to identify with His faithful work on their behalf in it.

A worldwide tradition for Palm Sunday is to save, year-round, the blessed palms from the procession. The congregation takes home these symbols of God's blessing, to adorn their homes or gardens. A favorite custom is to weave the palms into crosses, baskets, or bouquets. Then, in time for the beginning of Lent the next year, churches collect the dried palms and burn them to make the ashes for the Ash Wednesday services.

Based on the Jewish custom of ritual cleaning for Passover, rigorous spring-cleaning of the home traditionally occurs during the early days (Monday through Wednesday) of Holy Week. In the church, the preparatory cleaning for Easter includes the washing of the altar, communion table, or other furnishings, often observed on Holy Thursday.

After the services of Holy Thursday, for the traditional watch with Christ, parishioners in many cities around the world visit the altars at each of their nearby churches. Maria von Trapp beautifully describes this practice as known in Austria but observed commonly in Mexico, Spain, Portugal, and elsewhere:

> ... a replica of the Holy Sepulchre had been set up with more or less historical accuracy, with more or less taste, but always with the best of will. Like the crèche around Christmas time, so the Holy Sepulchre would be an object of pride for every parish... There would be a guard of honor, not only of the soldiers, but also of firemen in uniform and of war veterans with picturesque plumed hats. I still remember the atmosphere of holy awe stealing over my little heart when as a child I would make the rounds of churches.[4]

Dramatic commemorations of Christ's death absorb entire cities on Good Friday. Intense devotions starting midday mark The Three Hours' Agony of Christ on the cross (a tradition that started in Lima, Peru). During these hours, various cities hold funeral processions for Christ, with all the solemnity of a state funeral. At 3:00pm in Braga, Portugal, for example, cannons in 12 locations across the city fire simultaneously, vividly calling every inhabitant to attention at the hour of Jesus' death. Crowds march with ornate

4 Maria Von Trapp, *Around the Year with the Trapp Family* (New York, NY: Pantheon Books, 1955).

and often very old tableaux for the Stations of the Cross. In Seville, carvings from the 1500s are still used. Performances of the Good Friday readings, known as Passion Plays and once popular in Medieval Europe, still survive in some modern cities. The city of Oberammergau in Germany holds a Passion Play every ten years in honor of the pledge the residents made in 1633 to thank God for sparing their city from the effects of the bubonic plague. The world-famous Oberammergau Passion Play does not coincide with Holy Week but still preserves the tradition of portraying dramatically the passion of Christ.

On Holy Saturday (or on Easter Sunday) in various countries, parish priests make house visits to impart Easter blessings. Families ardently prepare their homes and elaborate baskets of food for these cherished visits.

In the Kitchen

Holy Week includes strict fasting days, such as Good Friday and Holy Saturday, along with the traditional feast days of Palm Sunday and Maundy Thursday. This list highlights a few of the traditional foods that symbolize the scenes of Holy Week:

For Palm Sunday

Fig pudding, to commemorate Matthew 21:19.

Pease porridge, or split-pea soup, marking the near-end of Lent (related to the penitential practice of wearing a pea in your shoe).

For Holy Thursday

Spring herb soup and spinach with fried eggs, green foods for lunch on *Gruendonnerstag*, Green Thursday. (In Austria, Holy Thursday is called *Gruendonnerstag* or "Green Thursday." "Gruen" does not stand for the color but instead derives from the ancient German word "greinen" meaning "to cry or moan." Nevertheless, the tradition on *Gruendonnerstag* is to eat green herbs and vegetables for lunch.)

Bitter herbs (parsley, chives, and celery greens) and unleavened bread, in reminiscence of the Passover meal.

Judases (*Jidáše*), pretzels or rolls shaped like a rope, a Czech tradition.

Dessert, since this is a feast day to honor the Lord's Supper.

For Good Friday

Hot cross buns, the traditional English bun eaten only on Good Friday.
A simple, gravy-based soup, to honor the Good Friday fast.

For the Very Young

Take the children to church. Worshipping together as a family leaves a
lasting impact on children. In a diary from a fourth-century pilgrim to
Jerusalem, we learn that Holy Week included the young and old, even
for the late and lengthy vigils.[5] No doubt services will conflict with
naps or bedtimes, so just showing up becomes a sacrifice. However, the
presence of children in the services blesses the entire community with
a visible reminder of the whole body of Christ. No one is too young or
unwelcome for these once-a-year celebrations.

Pack for Church:

*Prepare ahead of time for the children's needs so that everyone
can attend the services. Maybe this means packing a favorite
blanket in case the child falls asleep. Give the children paper and
ask them to draw what they see. For some children, doodling helps
release energy so they can better focus while sitting. Bring a special bag to church with items to occupy the children during the
sermons or quiet prayers. You can search, download, and print
your own Holy Week coloring pages from your home computer.*

Involve children in the services. The Holy Week traditions lend
themselves to children's participation. For example, just like the children of Jerusalem hurried to join Jesus' welcoming party, children today also become enchanted by the opportunity to wave long leaves
in the Palm Sunday parade. Maria von Trapp engaged her children's
interest by asking them to notice what was unique about each day's
service. Lively family discussions followed, as the children eagerly vol-
unteered their observations on the various colors, smells, and actions

---

5 *Egeria's Travels.* John Wilkinson, trans. (Oxford, UK: Aris & Phillips, 1999).

they had experienced.

Let the children imitate what they see at church. Children will naturally bring home what they view in the services. Stand back, letting them play on their own and recreate their own Holy Week scenes. You might catch them parading with palms through the backyard or washing each other's feet. Their enthusiasm for the traditions will deepen your own appreciation as well.

Appropriately mark at home the occasions you miss at church. Ideally our home devotions should not displace the wealth that the local church offers, but attending every service may not be possible. Instead, keep the spirit of the day. Some traditions more than others lend themselves to representing in a home setting. For example, a home group can wash each other's feet or spend an hour in vigil together, praying, singing hymns, and reading the relevant scripture passages. Set up the Stations of the Cross around the home or garden. The *Triduum* tradition of *Tenebrae* (Latin for "darkness") can provide the theme for bedtime prayers, with each person extinguishing candles after participating in a prayer or short reading.

Encourage discussion. Children love asking why. Take time to listen to their questions, and gently encourage them to share their impressions. Tell the stories of the traditions, and mirror their wonder at the richness of the season. Observe their play and make a note of the themes that capture their imaginations, being careful not to jump in with your own commentary. Sensitively weave into your everyday discussions the importance of the day and of how God demonstrates his love. Educate yourself so you can guide them through their questions, teaching them but also exemplifying through your life the meaning of our celebrations.

Listen to the Holy Week music together. Children love music and often effortlessly memorize the songs they hear. Many of the traditional Holy Week chants are simple plainsong, readily accessible to young, untrained ears. You may discover a few favorites that become suitable as lullabies, such as the *Pange Lingua.*

Make the celebrations a family affair. With patience and a sense of humor, handicrafts and cooking projects can be adapted for little hands. Together read the storybooks and look at the artwork to make this season come alive for the entire household.

Things to Make

Tell the story of Holy Week through arts and crafts. Your creations become things of beauty, aids for meditation, tools for teaching, memorable keepsakes, and enjoyable activities. Use whatever materials you find handy, in whatever medium you prefer. The means are endless: draw, paint, color, fold, cut, sculpt, carve, stitch, weave, bake, build, print, film, or collect your images. Using your favorite artistic technique, you can turn them into decorations, ornaments, centerpieces, banners, cards, pins, magnets, pictures, collages, mementos, wall art, scrapbooks, puppets, or dioramas. For example, weave your palm branches into crosses, or fashion your own stations of the cross. These visual depictions also become prayer aids that reinforce the meaning of the season. Consider the gospel scenes of Holy Week, take a look at this list of symbols, and give freedom to your own ingenuity:

Palm Branches (Mark 11:7–8, John 12:13)
Money bag and silver coins (Matt. 21:12 and 26:14–16)
Bread and Cup (Matt. 26:26–30, Luke 22:42)
Basin and Towel (John 13:3–5)
Rope (John 18:12, Matt. 27:5)
Rooster (Mark 14:72)
Scourge and Pillar (Mark 15:15, John 19:1)
Purple Robe (Mark 15:17–18)
Crown of Thorns (John 19:2, Mark 15:17–18)
Cross (John 19:16–18)
The Seamless Garment (John 19:23–24)
Nails (John 20:24–25)
Sponge (Matt. 27:48)
Lance (John 19:34)
Stone (Matt. 27:59–61)

Beyond the Home

During Holy Week, extend an invitation to your neighbors and co-workers to join you for church on Easter Sunday. Christmas and Easter might be the only times that some families attend church, so welcome them to yours.

Bake the traditional Good Friday hot cross buns for your neighborhood, school, or workplace. Sharing food gives you an instant conversation-starter to remind them what day it is and to entertain their questions.

Host a movie night. Friends who are unfamiliar with the scriptures may not agree to join you for church services but might feel more welcome in your home. Introduce the story of Christ's passion by watching and discussing a film together. Some options include *The Passion of the Christ* (2004, Rated R), *The Miracle Maker* (2000, suitable for children), and *Jesus of Nazareth* (1977, widely translated). After the 2004 film, various Christian apologists wrote guides for group discussion based on the movie themes. One such book, *Experiencing the Passion of Jesus,* by Lee Strobel and Garry Poole, does not have to accompany a movie-showing but can also stand alone as a good facilitation tool for question-and-answer sessions about Christ's death and resurrection.

Bring your friends to an art museum. Many museums contain a sacred art collection of images that correspond to Jesus' life and death. The shared experience of contemplating art, besides being a fun outing to enjoy together, also opens doors for discussing the relevance of Christ's complete self-offering.

Bring a meal to your pastor or clergy, or facilitate a meal delivery rotation to provide them food for Holy Week and Easter week. This busy time of year for the church ministers means that they are often exhausted during and after the *Triduum.* Your practical service will support them considerably. You may also consider offering to help decorate your church for Easter.

Share the wealth. The activity ideas from this chapter are not exclusive to your own home. Whatever interests you, whether to make or bake or enjoy, share among your community. For example, if you print out some hymn cards for your pocket, give a copy to your friends as well. Pass around the books or music that you collect for Holy Week. Bake in bulk and swap goods. Invite other families along to a craft session for children, or hold your activities at the local homeless shelter. Combine forces and efforts within your church to reach out to others near and far, in imitation of Christ. The young and old, the rich and poor, the homeless or imprisoned, can all be included in the daily activities that accompany our celebrations of the church year.

Resources

Seasonal Scripture Readings

Passion Narratives: Matthew 26–27, Mark 14–15, Luke 22–23, John 18–19.

Palm Sunday: Matthew 21:1–11; Mark 11:1–11; Luke 19:28–40; Psalm 118:1–2, 19–29; Isaiah 45:21–25, 50:4–9a; Philippians 2:5–11.

Maundy Thursday: Psalm 78:14–20, 23–25, 116:1–2, 10–17; Exodus 12:1–14; I Corinthians 11:23–26; John 13:1–17, 31–35.

Maundy Thursday Watch: Psalm 113–118; John 13–17.

Good Friday: Psalm 22, 40:1–14, 69:1–23; Isaiah 52:13–53:12; Hebrews 10:1–25 or 4:14–16, 5:7–9; John 18–19.

Holy Saturday: Psalm 31:1–4,15–16 or 131; Job 14:1–14 or Lamentations 3:1–9,19–24; I Peter 4:1–8; Matthew 27:57–66 or John 19:38–42.

Suggestions for Memorization:

Greater love has no one than this, that someone lay down his life for his friends. — John 15:13

…but emptied himself, by taking the form of a servant, being born in the likeness of men. And being found in human form, he humbled himself by becoming obedient to the point of death, even death on a cross. Therefore God has highly exalted him and bestowed on him the name that is above every name, so that at the name of Jesus every knee should bow, in heaven and on earth and under the earth, and every tongue confess that Jesus Christ is Lord, to the glory of God the Father.
…that by any means possible I may attain the resurrection from the dead. — Philippians 2:7–11, 3:11

And calling the crowd to him with his disciples, he said to them, "If anyone would come after me, let him deny himself and take up his cross and follow me." — Mark 8:34

I have been crucified with Christ. It is no longer I who live, but Christ who lives in me. And the life I now live in the flesh I live by faith in the Son of God, who loved me and gave himself for me.

But far be it from me to boast except in the cross of our Lord Jesus Christ, by which the world has been crucified to me, and I to the world. — *Galatians 2:20, 6:14*

Do you not know that all of us who have been baptized into Christ Jesus were baptized into his death? We were buried therefore with him by baptism into death, in order that, just as Christ was raised from the dead by the glory of the Father, we too might walk in newness of life.

For if we have been united with him in a death like his, we shall certainly be united with him in a resurrection like his. We know that our old self was crucified with him in order that the body of sin might be brought to nothing, so that we would no longer be enslaved to sin.

You, however, are not in the flesh but in the Spirit, if in fact the Spirit of God dwells in you. Anyone who does not have the Spirit of Christ does not belong to him. But if Christ is in you, although the body is dead because of sin, the Spirit is life because of righteousness. If the Spirit of him who raised Jesus from the dead dwells in you, he who raised Christ Jesus from the dead will also give life to your mortal bodies through his Spirit who dwells in you.

So then, brothers, we are debtors, not to the flesh, to live according to the flesh. For if you live according to the flesh you will die, but if by the Spirit you put to death the deeds of the body, you will live. For all who are led by the Spirit of God are sons of God. — *Romans 6:3–6, 8:9–14*

For to this you have been called, because Christ also suffered for you, leaving you an example, so that you might follow in his steps.

He himself bore our sins in his body on the tree, that we might die to sin and live to righteousness. By his wounds you have been healed. — *I Peter 2:21, 24*

Songs of the Season

The Holy Week journey is incomplete without music. Throughout church history, beautiful musical settings accompany the scripture readings and prayers offered at the Holy Week services, and many composers continue to find inspiration in the themes of Christ's suffering. The musical fare of this week is rich and voluminous. During the *Triduum* services of today we can hear some of the oldest sacred melodies still in use. Recordings are readily available locally and online, through iTunes and elsewhere, searchable by the composer's name and song title. Whether you listen to your church choir or to a recording at home, this music cultivates a transcendent meditation on the profundity of Christ's passion. Here is your Holy Week soundtrack.

Orchestral Compositions:

George Frideric Handel, *Messiah*. Part II of this famous English oratorio incorporates the scriptural texts and prophecies relating to the passion, death, and resurrection of Christ.

Johann Sebastian Bach, *The St. Matthew Passion* and *The St. John's Passion*. Bach's oratorios present the gospel texts of the Passion. Throughout the *St. Matthew* Passion he weaves the traditional hymn setting for "O Sacred Head Sore Wounded". Originally in German, English versions are also available.

Joseph Haydn, *The Seven Last Words of Christ*. Haydn's musical setting accompanies the seven "last words" of Christ, the bible verses of the short phrases Jesus uttered while on the cross, as recorded in the four gospels. There are many other settings to the "Seven Last Words" including one from the contemporary Scottish composer James MacMillan.

Gustav Holst, *The Prelude to The Hymn of Jesus*. Holst incorporates the traditional Passiontide hymns, *Vexilla Regis* and *Pange Lingua, Crux Fidelis*. (Tomás Luis de Victoria, Giovanni Pierluigi da Palestrina, and many others also composed musical settings to these *Triduum* hymns. Try especially the *Crux Fidelis* version by Joao IV, King John of Portugal.)

John Stainer, *The Crucifixion*. His Passiontide Oratorio in English is subtitled: *A Meditation on the Sacred Passion of the Holy Redeemer*.

Giovanni Battista Pergolesi, *Stabat Mater*. The *Stabat Mater* has inspired many musical settings throughout history (for example: Giovanni Pierluigi da Palestrina, Alessandro Scarlatti, Domenico Scarlatti, Antonio Vivaldi, Joseph Haydn, Franz Schubert, Gioacchino Rossini, Antonin Dvořák, Guiseppe Verdi, and others). Pergolesi's music also accompanies a one-act ballet by Peter Martins, which is a moving meditation on mourning.

Tomás Luis de Victoria, *Lamentations*. Victoria's sacred music includes settings of the Lamentations of Jeremiah for the Maundy Thursday, Good Friday, and Holy Saturday services. There are other settings of the Lamentations for the *Triduum*, including music by Giovanni Pierluigi da Palestrina, Thomas Tallis, and William Byrd.

Ralph Vaughan Williams, *Fantasia on Theme by Thomas Tallis*. The tune recollects a Holy Week chant "To mock your reign" with words by Fred Pratt Green.

John Tavener, *Lamentations and Praises*. This contemporary composer paints in music the biblical scenes of Holy Week.

Cindy Morgan, *The Loving Kind*. Another contemporary artist meditates on the events of Holy Week.

Liturgical Anthems:

Tenebrae Facta Sunt; Christus Factus Est; Ecce Vidimus Eum. These titles are the Latin translations for the Holy Week scripture readings of Luke 23:44, Philippians 2:8, and Isaiah 53:3, respectively. Johann Ernst Eberlin has beautiful settings for *Tenebrae Facta Sunt* and *Christus Factus Est*. Gregorian chant recordings also include these titles.

Gloria, Laus et Honor; Ubi Caritas; Pange Lingua, Crux Fidelis; Vexilla Regis; Stabat Mater; Ave Verum Corpus; Adoramus Te; Ecce lignum Crucis; Anima Christi. These devotional hymns of Holy Week have many musical settings that are known by their Latin titles. Or you can search for them according to their first lines translated below. Some of these titles also feature in Taizé chants, which are especially suitable for children.

Gloria, Laus et Honor, Processional for Palm Sunday (Latin, Theodulph of Orleans c.820). First line: "All glory, laud, and honor..."

Ubi Caritas, Ancient Anthem for the Washing of Feet. First line: "Where true charity and love are..."

Pange Lingua, Crux Fidelis, Processional for Good Friday (Latin, Venantius Fortunatus 530–609). First line: "Sing, my tongue, the glorious battle..."

Vexilla Regis, Processional for Holy Week (Latin, Venantius Fortunatus 530–609). First line: "The royal banners forward go..."

Stabat Mater, Hymn used on Good Friday (13th cen. Latin). First line:

"At the Cross her station keeping…"

Ave Verum Corpus, used for the Maundy Thursday Watch (14th cen. Latin). First line: "Hail, true Body, born of Mary…"

Adoramus Te, Ancient Anthem for Good Friday: "We adore you O Christ and we bless you, because by your holy cross you have redeemed the world."

Ecce lignum Crucis, Chant for Good Friday. First line: "Behold the wood of the Cross…"

Anima Christi, Prayer for the Lord's Supper. First line: "Soul of Christ, sanctify me…"

Hymn by John Henry Newman from "The Dream of Gerontius" (put to music by Edward Elgar). First line: "O generous love! that He, who smote…"

Hymn by Thomas Aquinas (1227–74), used on Maundy Thursday. First line: "Of the glorious body telling…"

"O Sacred Head, Sore Wounded", used for meditation during Holy Week (14th cen. Latin).

Hymn by Isaac Watts (1674–1748) for the Lord's Supper, used on Good Friday. First line: "When I survey the wondrous cross…"

Look through your church hymnal for other favorites such as: "Were you there when they crucified my Lord?" An iTunes search for "Music for Holy Week" also yields options of Byzantine chants.

Famous Artwork for Holy Week

Fra Angelico, *Crucifixion scene* (in Museo di San Marco, Florence), c.1437–1446.

Francesco Botticini, *The Crucifixion* (Predella Panel from an Altarpiece), c.1440–60.

Hieronymus Bosch, *Christ Mocked (The Crowning with Thorns)*, c.1490–1500.

Raphael, *The Mond Crucifixion (Altarpiece: The Crucified Christ with the Virgin Mary, Saints and Angels)*, c.1502–3.

Grünewald, Matthias, *Isenheim Altarpiece*, c.1512–1516.

Michelangelo Buonarotti, T*he Crucifixion with the Virgin and St John*, c.1555–64; Pietà.

El Greco, *Christ on the Cross*, c.1610; Agony in the Garden, c.1588.

Diego Velázquez, *Cristo crucificado*, 1632.

Salvador Dali, *Christ of Saint John of the Cross*, 1951.

Seasonal Reading

Poetry:

"The Dream of the Rood" (c.8th cen.).

"The Lament of the Virgin," from *The Lauds*, by Jacopone da Todi (c.1230–1306).

"*Verbum Crucis*," Paulinus of Nola (353–431).

"Good Friday: the Third Nocturne," by Peter Abelard (1079–1142).

Holy Sonnets and Sermons by John Donne (1572–1631).

"The Sacrifice," *The Temple*, by George Herbert (17th cen.).

"The Wreck of the Deutschland," by Gerard Manley Hopkins (19th cen.).

"A Better Resurrection," by Christina Rossetti (19th cen.).

"East Coker IV," by TS Eliot (20th cen.).

"*Corona benignitatis anni Dei*," by Paul Claudel.

"*Tenebrae*," by Geoffrey Hill.

"*Tenebrae*" and "The Descent," by David Gascoyne (1916–2001).

"Maundy Thursday" and *Sonnets for Stations of the Cross*, by Malcom Guite (21st cen.).

"Philomena," by John Peckham (13th cen. Archbishop of Canterbury).

Piers Plowman.

"*Salvator Mundi: Via Crucis*," by Denise Levertov.

Books:

The Man Born to Be King, by Dorothy Sayers.

The Case for Easter: Journalist Investigates the Evidence for the Resurrection, by Lee Strobel.

Judgement at Chelmsford, by Charles Williams.

The Revelations of Divine Love, by Julian of Norwich.

"The Scriptures, the Cross and the Power of God" a collection of sermons for every day of Holy Week, by N.T. Wright.

Simply Jesus, by N.T. Wright.

Jesus of Nazareth, Holy Week: From the Entrance into Jerusalem to the Resurrection, by Pope Benedict XVI.

Saving Belief, A Celebration of Faith, and Lord I Believe, by Austin Farrer.

The Jesus We Missed: The Surprising Truth about the Humanity of Christ by Patrick Henry Reardon.

Many other authors explore themes of redemptive suffering, including

J.R.R. Tolkien, C.S. Lewis, Charles Williams, George MacDonald, J.K. Rowling, Fyodor Dostoyevsky, Leo Tolstoy, Charlotte Bronte, William Shakespeare, Jane Austen, Shusaku Endo, Susan Howatch, Flannery O'Connor, and Aleksandr Solzhenitsyn.

Ancient Sources:

Melito of Sardis, *Office of Readings for Thursday of Holy Week* (2ⁿᵈ cen.).

St. Cyril of Jersualem, *On the Passion of Our Lord Jesus Christ* (4th cen.).

An Ancient Homily, The Lord Descends into Hell (Office of Readings for Holy Saturday).

Egeria's Travels (4th Cen.), translated by J. Wilkinson.

Prayers

Ancient Irish Prayer:

> O King of the Friday
> Whose limbs were stretched on the cross,
> O Lord who did suffer
> The bruises, wounds, the loss,
> We stretch ourselves
> Beneath the shield of thy might,
> Some fruit from the tree of thy passion
> Fall on us this night!

Prayer of the Benedictine nuns of Chichester, fifteenth century:

> O Jesu let me never forget thy bitter passion
> That thou sufferest for my transgression
> For in thy blessed wounds is the very school
> That must teach me with the world to be called a fool.

Byzantine Triparion for the Maundy Thursday Eucharist:

> Receive me today, O Son of God, as a partaker of thy Mystic Feast;
> for I will not speak of the Mystery to thine enemies;
> I will not kiss thee as did Judas;
> but as the thief I will confess thee;
> Lord, remember me when thou comest in thy Kingdom.

Gloria, Laus et Honor, *ninth century Hymn for the Palm Sunday Pro-*

cession:

> All glory, laud and honor,
> To Thee, Redeemer, King,
> To Whom the lips of children
> Made sweet hosannas ring.

> Thou art the King of Israel,
> Thou David's royal Son,
> Who in the Lord's Name comest,
> The King and Blessèd One.

Common Prayer for the beginning of Holy Week:

Assist us mercifully with your help, O Lord God of our salvation, that we may enter with joy upon the contemplation of those mighty acts, whereby you have given us life and immortality; through Jesus Christ our Lord. Amen.[6]

Ancient Latin Anthem for the Washing of the Feet:

> *Ubi caritas et amor, Deus ibi est.*
> God is love, and where true love is, God himself is there.

---

6 *Book of Common Prayer (1986)*, 270.

Easter

by Lindsay Marshall

Introduction to Easter

Easter is the culmination of the rest of the church year, the yearly celebration of Christ's resurrection. The season stretches across, in the words of the *Book of Common Prayer*,[1] "His blessed passion and precious death, His mighty resurrection and glorious ascension." Its chief focus is on the saving power of Christ over death and the historical event of His resurrection. It's a season of excess with feasting, song, and more alleluias than any reasonable person would try to fit into one church service at a time. In short, it is roughly six weeks of unbridled, unfettered, unfiltered joy: praise and thanksgiving to our mighty Savior, and ecstatic celebration of the hope we have in His victory over death.

Scripture is relatively light on the events that pass between Christ's resurrection and His ascension to heaven. Like all good storytellers, the gospel writers knew that once the climax of the story has happened, the rest is just falling action. But sparse in plot as it is, that falling action is wonderful, and it has some of the most poignant and personal moments in the gospel accounts. As the four gospel writers tell the story, early in the morning on Easter Sunday, Mary Magdalene and the other women arrive to find the tomb empty, an angel telling them to tell the disciples that Christ has risen, just as He said. But John gives us more detail. Mary lingers in the graveyard. She wants to see for herself, so she peers into the tomb. Two angels sit where the body lay, and ask her why she is weeping. "They have taken away my Lord," she replies. Then a voice behind her asks why she's weeping, who she seeks. She begs to know where this strange man has taken her beloved teacher. And then He says her name, and she knows Him (John 20). He calls His sheep by name, and His sheep know His voice, indeed.

---

1 1986 version.

Likewise, the Easter season reminds us of the account of the road to Emmaus. Again, Christ appears incognito, and though, according to Luke, "Beginning with Moses and all the Prophets, He interpreted to them in all the Scriptures the things concerning Himself," the disciples don't realize who He is until after He's left (24:27). Christ's almost comical encounters with doubting disciples in the upper room lend authentic emotion to the mystical event.

John, always fascinated by the relationships between Christ and His followers, gives us another deeply personal account. After Christ has appeared to the disciples, including Thomas, they're back where He found them, out fishing. After a fruitless night of work, He appears on the beach and shouts to them, "Children, do you have any fish?" (John 21:5). They, yet again failing to recognize Him, say no, and He tells them to drop their nets on the other side of the boat. It's a ridiculous request of seasoned fishermen, but they do, and when the nets so teem with fish they can't haul them over the side, Peter grabs his cloak and leaps into the water, fighting through the sea to get to the Lord. The risen Lord makes them breakfast on the beach, and offers Peter His chance to redeem His denials on the night of the crucifixion. Three times He asks, "Simon, son of John, do you love Me?" (21:15–17) and three times, Peter answers yes. And each time, Jesus gives Peter the command that will determine the course not just of his life, but of the early church: "Feed my sheep" (21:17).

The Easter season ends, as do three of the four gospels, with the Ascension. Christ rises to heaven in the presence of many witnesses, instructing them to go into the world and share the gospel. John, ever focused on the relationship between believers and Christ, ends with Christ's admonition to Peter: "If it is my will that he remain until I come, what is that to you? You follow me!" (21:23).

That's the heartbeat of the Easter season. In all the pomp and glory of the festival, we are constantly reminded that, as Saint Augustine of Hippo said in *On Christian Teaching*, "We made bad use of immortality, and so we died; Christ made good use of mortality, and so we live."[2] All we must do now is follow Him.

Calendar

Easter is rare among the Christian holy days because it is celebrat-

2 Augustine of Hippo, *On Christian Teaching*, R.P.H. Green, trans. (New York, NY: Oxford University Press, 2008), I.29.

ed in the same time of year as the event it commemorates. The early church used the timing of feast days to teach the unreached and the next generation major tenets of the faith. Christmas fell to the winter solstice to emphasize Christ as beginning of life eternal in the dead time of the year. All Saints Eve and Day correspond with Samhain and Pomona's festival, reminding us that in our remembrance of the dead comes communion of the saints. Easter, however, occurs in the same season that Jesus Christ was historically crucified by Rome. That gives us an annual opportunity, unique among major church festivals, to experience a remembrance of the major event of our salvation in the same time of year it historically occurred.

In the early days of the church, no celebration was more important than the Resurrection — and none was more controversial. As early as Paul's epistles, an argument grew over the nature of this new religious group. Were Christians the first of a new religion, or simply a sect of Jews who followed the teachings of Jesus as rabbi? This question put immense pressure on the early church, especially as Christian persecutions ended with Galerius's Edict of Toleration (AD 311), to use the celebration of the faith's greatest feast day to make clear the faith's claims about Christ.

Initially, Christians celebrated Easter in conjunction with Passover; this established Easter's identity as a moveable feast. But within a few short generations, as the church wrestled with Christological doctrine, congregations began to separate the celebration of Easter from Passover. Eventually, when a Christian community celebrated Easter became a litmus test for orthodoxy which, given the chaotic nature of the aftermath of Rome's fall in Western Europe, gave way to confusing episodes and bitter theological disputes.

The Venerable Bede recounts one case of confused identity in his *Ecclesiastical History of the English People* that occurred in the ancient British kingdom of Northumbria in the mid-7th century. One of the great strengths of the Roman Empire was its ability to maintain travel routes (and ensure relative safety upon them) throughout Europe, Northern Africa, and parts of Western Asia. When Christianity arrived in the first century, the infrastructure was in place to allow the new religion to spread rapidly. When Rome collapsed, however, it took a lot of that ease of travel and communication with it. Ireland found itself cut off from the rest of the church in the 5th century when Roman Britain was conquered by the Angles, Saxons, and Jutes. So the Irish church simply carried on as they had. But in the century that followed, the Roman church established a celebration of Easter distinct from the Jewish festival in order to reject the heresy that Christ was not the divine Messiah, but rather another prophet of the Jewish faith. When Pope Saint Gregory the Great's missionaries, making their way north from Kent and Saint Aedan's Irish missionaries heading south from Scotland bumped into each other in the border kingdom of Northumbria in AD 652, it caused quite an argument. The Romans assumed the Irish were defying the church's teaching on the divinity of Christ. The Irish were flabbergasted to find such an important holy day in dispute. King Oswy observed that "as they all expected the same kingdom in heaven, so they ought not to differ in the celebration of the Divine mysteries"[3] and called the Synod at Whitby to settle the matter. Rome's calendar won.

Another division occurred after the Great Schism of the Eastern and Western churches in AD 1054. Eastern and Western Christians celebrate Easter ("*Pascha*" in the Greek-based East) on different days not for theological argument, but by historical accident. The church in Rome adopted the Gregorian calendar because the old Julian calendar from Roman times had an error in its calculation of the vernal equinox. Left without Passover as a guide, the Christian church in the West calculated Easter from the vernal equinox. The Eastern church kept the Julian calendar but also adjusted Easter to correspond with the more accurate lunar calendar and made certain Easter always fell after the Jewish celebration of Passover (since Jesus was historically crucified over Passover). Sometimes both Easter celebrations coincide (and occasionally, they fall on Passover as well!). More often, the Western Easter precedes the Eastern *Pascha* by several weeks.

And thus we have a very confusing moveable feast. But the Easter season is the focal point of the entire church year. Advent starts the year, anticipating the incarnation, and we move through Epiphany to Lent recounting the gospel story, until we reach Holy Week, and remember the sacrifice that brings us eternal life. The rest of the calendar celebrates the blessings we receive from that sacrifice until we begin again with the start of Advent in late autumn. But even in that steady flow of shifting focal points, the Easter season is with the church all year. In the liturgical tradition, every weekend is a little Easter. Friday is always a remembrance of the crucifixion, and Sunday is always a celebration of the resurrection. Even during Lent, believers are expected

3 Bede (the Venerable), *Ecclesiastical History of the English People*, J.A. Giles, trans. (London, UK: George Bell & Sons, 1903), III.25.

to moderately break their fasts on Sundays to remember resurrection. The joy of our salvation is too great to smother even in the midst of preparing ourselves to experience it again.

It may seem strange for the most central holy day of the Christian calendar to be so embroiled in controversy, for its timing to be based on fighting off questions from early heresies spun from confused and incomplete doctrine. Why then should we stick to such a muddled calendar? Monsignor Peter Elliott gives a solid argument for it in his *Ceremonies of the Liturgical Year According to the Modern Roman Rite*:

> Choosing the "right" times to celebrate or fast were important to our forebears in the Faith. They regarded the calendar itself as a way of holding onto and passing on the apostolic tradition. Sacred time offered them a kind of "orthopraxis" that sustained their orthodoxy. This distant debate reminds us that we may fail to appreciate the power and precision of memory in the ancient world... ours is a historical religion and the historical basis of Christianity is reflected in the minds behind the early developments of the sacred calendar that became our Liturgical Year. They knew what some of us tend to forget, that Christianity stands or falls on the reality of specific events that occurred in the First Century. Close to those events, influenced by disciples of the first witnesses, they passed on those unique revelatory moments within the community of the Church, not only in Scripture and Tradition, in doctrines and sacraments but in the way they celebrated times and seasons.

In America, we still hold national elections on Tuesdays because in the late 18th century, farmers brought their goods to town on Tuesdays in preparation for Wednesday markets. If it meant so much, for such greater reason, to our spiritual ancestors to celebrate Easter as a moveable feast, we can learn a lot about our heritage of faith by keeping the feast as they did.

The Traditions

The Great Vigil
Because the ancients marked the end of one day and beginning of the next at sundown, Easter technically begins at sundown on Holy Saturday. Scripture is unclear on the exact timing of the resurrection,

but we know that Christ was laid in the tomb in a hurry before sundown on Good Friday and first appeared to the women when they returned to anoint the body after the Sabbath on Sunday morning. The early church assumed, therefore, that the harrowing of hell happened sometime in the night before His appearance to the women in the garden. And thus began what Saint Augustine called "the mother of all vigils." Just as Christ asked His disciples to watch and pray with Him in Gethsemane, we wait with Him as we await the celebration of His return from death.

The earliest records of the Great Vigil come from a manuscript held by the Armenian Patriarchate of Jerusalem. It lists 12 readings from Scripture that lead the people through a litany of God's promises. It starts with the Creation account and includes the sacrifice of Isaac, the establishment of Passover, the story of Jonah, the Red Sea, the promise of Jerusalem's coming glory, God's answer to Job, Elijah's assumption, Jeremiah's renewal of covenant, Ezekiel's valley of dry bones, Israel's entry into the Promised Land, and the story of Shadrach, Meshach, and Abednego. In his *The Origins of the Liturgical Calendar*, Thomas J. Talley observes that these readings form the backbone of Christendom's understanding of the story of salvation from its earliest moments in the Garden.

The vigil service typically starts in the dark, with congregants carrying candles lit from the Paschal candle in a ceremony at the church door. The readings of the prophecies all occur in the dark, and as the readings come to the resurrection account, the congregation sings the *Gloria* for the first time since Lent began. Church lights come on, bells ring, and the *Triduum* is over. The celebration marks the early Christian belief that Christ rose from the grave sometime during the night before Easter. While some churches choose to hold the main celebration of the resurrection on Easter morning in order to replicate the experience of the women who first discovered the empty tomb, others follow the tradition of marking Christ's rising from the setting of the sun.

In the earliest days of the faith, believers guarded the community of Christ with great care. Wary of infiltrators who served as spies for a hostile Roman government and mindful of the risk conversion brought to new converts, the early Christians constructed a system of mentorship, sponsorship, and education before baptism to ensure new converts were genuine in their desire for baptism and knew what they were getting themselves into by doing it. This system lasted well into the 6ᵗʰ century in Western Europe, and the Great Vigil was the logical time to complete the sacrament. From Maundy Thursday through Good Friday, they kept vigil, staying up all night in prayer in the church. Baptism was conferred on Holy Saturday, and their first communion as brothers and sisters in Christ happened after sundown during the Great Vigil.

Easter Sunday

Despite the fact that this is the highest holy day of the church year, Easter morning can be a little anti-climatic after the majesty of the Great Vigil. But Christ is risen, and Easter Sunday is the day to pull out all the stops and shout it from the rooftops. Bells, alleluias, hats, and lilies traditionally grace the service, along with the happy refrain "Christ is risen! He is risen indeed!" For the early church, Easter was more than the time of year to remember Christ's victory over death. It was a time to welcome new people into the body, and a time to re-member why, embattled as they were, they had hope. For those of us living post-Constantine, it launches us into the rest of the church year, reminding us of the joy that compels us to worship Him.

Easter Sunday also marks the beginning of the 50 days of the Easter season. Though the life of the church marches along as usual, it does so peppered with extra alleluias. The season from Easter Sunday until Ascension focuses on Christ's appearances to His disciples and other events of His post-resurrection time on earth. As Saint John said in his Gospel, "We have seen his glory, glory as of the only Son from the Father, full of grace and truth" (John 1:14). That glory, unfiltered by the sorrow of the road to the Cross, is the central theme of the Easter season.

The Visitation

Because the church only has one year to tell all its stories, sometimes feasts from different seasons overlap. The Annunciation, Gabriel's an-nouncement to Mary that she would be the one to carry Christ into our realm, necessarily precedes Christmas by nine months, and so it occurs during Lent. Likewise, Scripture tells us that Mary later went to stay with her cousin Elizabeth, who was carrying John the Baptist at the time. The medieval church added the observance of this visit to the calendar to help teach believers about Mary's role as *theotokos*, "God-bearer". And, as the early church fathers believed, any statement about Mary is really a statement about her Son, the feast reminds us of His identity as well. This especially came in handy when, during the early days of the church, the confusion over Christ's identity as fully God and fully man erupted into numerous heresies. The Church found that establishing Mary's identity as *theotokos* affirmed Christ's divinity and humanity in one clear, relatable image.

The story is found in the gospel of Luke (1:39–56). After learning of her own pregnancy, Mary goes to stay with her relatives, Zechariah and Elizabeth. Gabriel told her that her aunt Elizabeth, thought to be barren, was with child. When Mary greets Elizabeth, "The baby leaped in her womb." The Spirit tells Elizabeth that all Mary will tell her is true, and the older woman worships God. Mary is so overwhelmed by the greeting, she prays one of the most famous prayers in the Gospel, the *Magnificat*.

The Feast of the Visitation is a minor feast within the Easter season with few of its own traditions, but it serves to drive the year forward. It reminds us, as the church calendar so often does, that the events we celebrate are intertwined. We can't have the joy of Easter without the humility of the incarnation.

The Ascension

The culmination of the Easter season is Christ's last recorded act on earth: His ascension into heaven. Mark and Luke record Christ's ascension (Luke does so twice, in his Gospel and in the book of Acts), and in both cases, it immediately follows Christ's charge to His disciples to "go into all the world and proclaim the Gospel to the whole creation" (Mark 16:15a). It marks the fortieth day from Easter Sunday, so it, too, is a moveable feast and it, too, falls on different dates for the Western and Eastern churches. Traditionally the feast falls on a Thursday, so it is sometimes referred to in the Anglican church as Holy Thursday, but because countries in the West stopped declaring that day a national holiday, most churches petitioned to move the feast to the following Sunday, and the Ascension is widely celebrated on a Sunday in North America and in Europe.

The Ascension is a feast that has fallen from its level of importance in the modern age. Though we don't know how the observance began, most early church scholars agree the apostles must have begun the celebration themselves due to its universality by the 5th century. Early in the life of the church, it was upheld with the same importance as the incarnation, the passion, the resurrection, and Pentecost. For the early and medieval church, it heralded two vital moments of salvation history: the final blow to Satan and the power of death, and the entry of humanity into heaven. Christ went to prepare a place for us, and He sits on the right hand of the Father as our advocate. The church celebrated these truths through pageants, processions, and occasionally by having a tiny figure of Jesus pulled up and out of the church through a hole in the roof.

New Traditions

The goal of the Easter season is to let the joy of the season filter every pattern of daily life. Early Christians greeted each other with alleluias and the common call and response "Christ is risen!" "The Lord is risen indeed!" They spent their time feasting together, dancing, singing, sharing each other's joys and above all spending time together as community. Think about how your family might incorporate the spirit of that historical celebration into this season. Throw a party! Make Easter dinner a festive occasion, not an obligatory extended family gathering. Don't let it stop on Easter Sunday. In the Orthodox tradition, the week following Easter is called Bright Week, and it's spent visiting friends and family and, each night, feasting!

Take a page from the early church. Early in church history, Easter traditions started to mirror pagan spring festivals. The idea was to use the language of the surrounding culture to communicate the gospel. In the spring, pagan religions of Western Europe and the Middle East held fertility festivals to celebrate new life. Early Christians borrowed symbols from those festivals (eggs, bunnies, etc.) as a way to transform what were typically celebrations of base desire and show a greater life was possible. If fertility was worthy of feasting and partying, how much more so eternal life?

So do what the early church did. Celebrate life! Go for a hike. Spend time outside drinking in the beauty of creation. Spring is usually the season for wildflowers. Go see them! Paint, write, sing, and dance. Let the joy of the season overflow.

The language of modern American culture is the language of cinema. Don't overlook the opportunity great film has for helping your family contemplate the mystery of the Resurrection. There are classics of course, like *The Robe* (1953), but don't limit yourself to the traditional narrative. Films like *The Passion of Joan of Arc* (1928), *Babette's Feast* (1987), and *Tree of Life* (2011) approach the celebration of the life we have in Christ in intense, innovative ways.

Attend a church outside your tradition. One of the most vital

111

messages of the resurrection is that it is Christ's sacrifice and triumph over death that binds us together as His body. If you've never been to a Great Vigil service, find one nearby and attend. If you attend a liturgical church and have never been to a Pentecostal service, Easter Sunday might be the biggest party you'll ever attend. If there's an Orthodox church nearby, consider attending *Pascha* (the Eastern Great Vigil). Stepping outside our traditions helps us see our faith with new eyes, and it's always good, especially on holy days, to remind ourselves that God is bigger than our denomination and connect with the larger Body of Christ.

Around the World

The Eastern Church
Celebrations of the Orthodox church are quite similar to those in the West, but with some key differences. For *Pascha*, the Orthodox version of the Great Vigil, members gather outside and light a new fire as well, but they process around the building singing the Paschal *troparion*:

> Christ is risen from the dead,
> Trampling down death by death,
> And upon those in the tombs
> Bestowing life!

The closed doors of the church represent the sealed tomb, and the priest opens them to mark the moment of Christ's resurrection.

Often the priest, after the liturgy, will bless baskets of boiled eggs. They've been dyed red to symbolize Christ's blood, and cracking them together symbolized breaking open the tomb. Then the congregation will usually share a massive feast to break the fast of Great Lent. The celebration usually doesn't end until at least 5 a.m.

Ethiopia
Tigist Gaddissa, from Addis Abada, Ethiopia, offered this account of how celebrations in her home country differ from American ones:

> Easter, "*Fasika*", is one of the biggest holidays for both Orthodox and Evangelical Christians in Ethiopia.
>
> On Saturday night both believers (evangelicals and Orthodox), spend the night at church praying, worshiping, listening to sermons, singing and dancing.

Early morning Sunday around 3:00am, the Orthodox believers return home and break their fast by eating chicken stew with *enjera* (typical traditional food Ethiopians eat on holidays). The evangelicals stay at church until 6:00am. Then, all believers go out of the sanctuary and make a big circle in the church compound. Each one of them put their candlelight on and sings songs of resurrection with traditional drums and instruments. All believers walk to their home with their candle-lights on, singing and dancing.

Late Sunday morning, evangelicals go back to church for more worship and sermon. In the afternoon, most families stay at home eating and having fun and fellowship with family, neighbors and relatives. It is customary for people to visit each other and feed each other traditional foods and drinks on Easter day.[4]

In the Kitchen

There are a lot of great ways to celebrate holidays with food, and food blogs and cooking channels go nuts publishing innovative ways to take advantage of seasonal treats. But one thing most Easter traditions around the globe have in common is a communal feast with family and friends. We remember that for Christmas, but sometimes forget that Easter isn't about eggs, chocolate bunnies, and a great rack of lamb with mint jelly. It's about rejoicing together, and sometimes the simplest meals with meaning taste better than anything on Epicurious.

In that spirit, I've asked my mother-in-law if I could share her recipe for our favorite treat: Easter bread.

Easter Bread, Robin Marshall

Ingredients
- 8 c. flour
- 9 eggs
- 1 large cake yeast or 3 pkgs. yeast
- ¾ stick oleo

---

4 From a conversation with the author.

- ½ t. anise extract *
- 1 c. sugar; add more if you want a sweeter bread
- ½ c. milk **
- 1 t. vanilla extract
- ¼ t. salt (if kosher, large granular, double)

Method

1. Melt oleo in milk, and dissolve yeast in 1/2 c. of water with a little sugar.
2. Beat eggs and sugar together, then add flour and the rest of the ingredients. This bread will need to rise three times. First rise is for 2 hours, then punch down and let rise 1 ½ hours, then punch down, and divide up into loaf pans, or braid, decorating with raw colored eggs, and allow to rise for 2 hours, or has doubled in size.
3. Bake at 350°, for approximately 30 minutes. This will depend on the size of your loaf pan, or braided bread.
4. Once you remove from the oven, immediately brush warm bread with melted butter.

This recipe will make 6 medium loaves.

Anise extract in this recipe will allow for a good nose, and a slight taste. For those that enjoy a little more taste, you can put in more extract, or anise oil. Taste can be evaluated by tasting the raw dough. For pregnant women, the consuming of raw eggs should be avoided.

**Milk, with all bread making, needs to reach a scald (just below boiling, about 180ºF) to destroy the enzyme that will inhibit a good rise in your bread. Make sure milk and oleo have reached room temperature prior to adding it to the other ingredients.*

For the Very Young

In keeping with the early church tradition of expanding traditional seasonal observance to explain Christian doctrine, you can use traditional seasonal observance to introduce your younger children to the reason we're celebrating.

To talk about the importance of new life, consider taking the children to a local farm or zoo. Observing animals, especially ones caring for their young, offers a natural and memorable way to talk about Christ's gift of life.

If you don't already attend a church with a liturgy that offers a children's sermon, it can be a great experience for small children, especially over Easter. The sounds, images, and interactive nature of the service not only draw children's attention, but because they were developed to guide illiterate believers in complex theology, they offer a great opportunity for children to inquire about big questions in terms they can understand.

When preparing meals for the family, consider including young children in safe, simple tasks. Making the preparations part of the experience rather than a behind-the-scenes prelude gives you the opportunity to offer young kids more insight into why we're celebrating the way we are and ask their questions.

Things to Make

There are the obligatory crafts associated with the season, of course, and there's a reason they're popular. Rich with symbolism and fun to make, crafts help children connect with the more esoteric ideas of the season. Dyed eggs are standard, but consider spicing them up a bit. Talk to your children about the symbolism behind different colors and have them choose the colors for their meaning as well as their beauty.

In Western Europe, it's customary to decorate trees in the town square by hanging dyed eggs from them. The effect can sometimes be bizarre, but could also be artfully done.

In some European cultures, setting bonfires are a part of traditional Easter celebrations. They commemorate the new light of the Paschal candle, but also end up being something of a competition for young men, mild pyromania seeming to be a cross-cultural trait of early adolescence. Either way, it's a great excuse for a cozy bonfire on the beach, in a fire-pit in the yard, at a park, or by a campsite.

The most lasting thing you could do could also be the most delicious. Planting a garden is a great way to involve every member of the family in an activity based on the theme of new life. The layers of symbolism never end: beauty, sustenance, growth, nourishment... there's a reason Christ used a lot of botanical imagery to illustrate the life of faith.

Beyond the Home

Just as with celebrating Easter with your family, follow the early church in reaching outside your home to our community. The twin great themes of the Easter season are life and freedom. The first believers let those blessings, bestowed on us by Christ's work on the cross, overflow in their lives and worked to bring life and freedom to those around them, even their persecutors. Your family can do the same.

Consider connecting with a local anti-trafficking organization. Human trafficking, modern slavery, is one of the most egregious human rights violations we face today. It is illegal everywhere, and it is present everywhere, from the supply chains of the food we purchase, the garments we wear, and the products we use, to the street corners of our cities, people are forced to work without pay under threat of violence so we can enjoy our creature comforts. A great irony of the Easter season is that in celebrating it (buying chocolate candy, new clothes for Easter Sunday), we often participate in oppression by demanding cheap products without asking why they can be so cheap. Becoming an educated consumer and seeking fairly-traded goods is a way to let Christ's gift of freedom from sin spill over into our lives and fight for physical freedom for others. (For more, visit notforsalecampaign.org or read *Everyday Justice* by Julie Goss Clawson.)

All life is sacred. Consider using this season as a time to help defend it. Contact your local crisis pregnancy center and volunteer. Volunteer at a battered women's shelter. Find out how you can donate to organizations that help the poor in your community, to provide subsistence or health care. Christ came that we might have life, and that we might have it abundantly. Seek ways to help your community thrive.

If the beauty of the natural world can show us deep theological truths, it makes sense to respond by being its stewards. Consider supporting conservation efforts. Our national parks are always in need of funding, and state and local parks even more so. They can also use volunteers. Check with your favorite local open space and see how your family can help foster life by caring for God's creation. It may even be as simple as volunteering at your local animal shelter. If His eye is always on the sparrow, surely it's also on dogs and cats abandoned by their owners.

Share Easter with the less fortunate. Many churches have ministries to the homeless, and some, like my home church, run church services for them. Ask your area churches if they have similar programs. When

Christ said, "You always have the poor with you," He didn't mean there would always be poor people; He meant that if we follow Him, we will always be found with the poor.

Resources

Seasonal Scripture Readings

Ephesians
Philippians 3:1–17
Philemon
Hebrews

Suggestions for Memorization:

And he came to Nazareth, where he had been brought up. And as was his custom, he went to the synagogue on the Sabbath day, and he stood up to read. And the scroll of the prophet Isaiah was given to him. He unrolled the scroll and found the place where it was written,
"The Spirit of the Lord is upon me,
because he has anointed me
to proclaim good news to the poor.
He has sent me to proclaim liberty to the captives
and recovering of sight to the blind,
to set at liberty those who are oppressed,
to proclaim the year of the Lord's favor."
And he rolled up the scroll and gave it back to the attendant and sat down. And the eyes of all in the synagogue were fixed on him. And he began to say to them, "Today this Scripture has been fulfilled in your hearing." — *Luke 4:16–21*

But Mary stood weeping outside the tomb, and as she wept she stooped to look into the tomb. And she saw two angels in white, sitting where the body of Jesus had lain, one at the head and one at the feet. They said to her, "Woman, why are you weeping?" She said to them, "They have taken away my Lord, and I do not know where they have laid him." Having said this, she turned around and saw Jesus standing, but she did not know that it was Jesus. Jesus said to her, "Woman, why are you weeping? Whom are you seeking?" Supposing him to be the gardener, she said to him, "Sir, if you have carried him away, tell me where you have laid him, and I will take him away." Jesus said to her, "Mary." She turned and said to him in Aramaic, "Rabboni!" (which means Teacher). Jesus said to her, "Do not cling to me, for I have not yet ascended to the Father; but go to my brothers and say to them, 'I am ascending to my Father and your Father, to my God and your God.'" Mary Magdalene went and announced to the disciples, "I have seen the Lord"—and that he had said these things to her. — John 20:11–18

In the beginning was the Word, and the Word was with God, and the Word was God. He was in the beginning with God. All things were made through him, and without him was not any thing made that was made. In him was life, and the life was the light of men. The light shines in the darkness, and the darkness has not overcome it.
There was a man sent from God, whose name was John. He came as a witness, to bear witness about the light, that all might believe through him. He was not the light, but came to bear witness about the light.
The true light, which gives light to everyone, was coming into the world. He was in the world, and the world was made through him, yet the world did not know him. He came to his own, and his own people did not receive him. But to all who did receive him, who believed in his name, he gave the right to become children of God, who were born, not of blood nor of the will of the flesh nor of the will of man, but of God.
And the Word became flesh and dwelt among us, and we have seen his glory, glory as of the only Son from the Father, full of grace and truth. — John 1:1–14

Seasonal Reading

For Children
What is Easter?, by Michelle Medlock Adams: This is an excellent resource for preschoolers to help them understand that yes, jellybeans
are awesome, but there's a lot more to this holiday than just that.

The Lion, the Witch, and the Wardrobe, by C.S. Lewis: This classic imagination of the work of salvation in another world is often more closely associated with Christmas than Easter, but the redemptive work
of the resurrection is Lewis's central theme.

For All Ages
Auralia's Colors, by Jeffrey Overstreet: The first of the series *The Auralia
Thread, Auralia's Colors* is excellent reading for Easter. The story centers on a young artist born into a world without color. Her attempt
to bring wonder and beauty to a kingdom of drab grays and browns
rocks the world of House Abascar and points to something greater
than all themselves.

For More Serious Reading
"Easter Wings," by George Herbert.

The *Dream of the Rood*.

"Sermon XLV," "The New Birth," by John Wesley.

"La Corona," "Holy Sonnet 6," and "Holy Sonnet 8," by John Donne.

"On The Resurrection of Christ," by William Dunbar.

"Seven Stanzas at Easter," by John Updike.

"On Belief in the Physical Resurrection of Jesus; Ascension; Ikon: The
Harrowing of Hell," by Denise Levertov.

Songs of the Season

This category could become so staggeringly large it's hardly worth beginning. Really, any song with an alleluia would do! But here are some
favorites, as well as a few that tend to get overlooked in favor of their
more popular colleagues.

Traditional Hymns
"The strife is o'er, the battle done," W.H. Monk, arr. Palestrina.

"Christians to the Paschal victim offer your thankful praises," plainsong.

"The head that once was crowned with thorns," J. Clark, Thomas Kelly.

"Now, my tongue, the mystery telling," plainsong.

"Christ the Lord is risen today," Wesley.
"I heard the voice of Jesus say," Horatius Bonar, T. Tallis.

Other Great Songs
"Easter Song," Keith Green.
"Love Crucified, Arose," Michael Card.
"Come to the Table," Michael Card.
"The Trumpet Child," Over the Rhine.

Prayers

Easter Evening

Grant, O Lord, that as we are baptized into the death of thy blessed Son, our Saviour Jesus Christ, so by continual mortifying our corrupt affections we may be buried with him; and that through the grave, and gate of death, we may pass to our joyful resurrection; for his merits, who died, and was buried, and rose again for us, the same thy Son Jesus Christ our Lord. Amen.[5]

Easter Day

Almighty God, who through thine only-begotten Son Jesus Christ hast overcome death, and opened unto us the gate of everlasting life; We humbly beseech thee that, as by thy special grace preventing us thou dost put into our minds good desires, so by thy continual help we may bring the same to good effect; through the same Jesus Christ our Lord, who liveth and reigneth with thee and the Holy Ghost ever, one God, world without end. Amen.[6]

- or this -

O God, who for our redemption didst give thine only-begotten Son to the death of the Cross, and by his glorious resurrection hast delivered us from the power of our enemy; Grant us so to die daily from sin, that we may evermore live with him in the joy of his resurrection; through the same thy Son Christ our Lord. Amen.[7]

---

5 *Book of Common Prayer (1928)*, 161
6 *Book of Common Prayer (1986)*, 170.
7 Ibid.

Other Easter Prayers

O God, whose blessed Son did manifest himself to his disciples in the breaking of bread; Open, we pray thee, the eyes of our faith, that we may behold thee in all thy works through the same thy Son Jesus Christ our Lord. Amen.[8]

- or this -

Grant, we beseech thee, Almighty God, that we who celebrate with reverence the Paschal feast, may be found worthy to attain to everlasting joys; through Jesus Christ our Lord. Amen.[9]

- or this -

O Lord, from whom all good things do come; Grant to us thy humble servants, that by thy holy inspiration we may think those things that are good, and by thy merciful guiding may perform the same; through our Lord Jesus Christ. Amen.[10]

- or this -

Grant, we beseech thee, Almighty God, that like as we do believe thy only-begotten Son our Lord Jesus Christ to have ascended into the heavens; so we may also in heart and mind thither ascend, and with him continually dwell, who liveth and reigneth with thee and the Holy Ghost, one God, world without end. Amen.[11]

---

8 *Book of Common Prayer (1986)*, 171.
9 Ibid.
10 *Book of Common Prayer (1928)*,175.
11 *Book of Common Prayer (1986)*, 174.

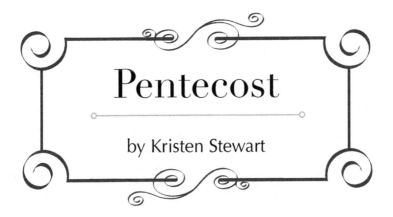

Pentecost

by Kristen Stewart

Introduction to Pentecost

After years of having Jesus with them, to teach and to guide them, the disciples watched Him ascend into heaven. As amazed as they were, they also found themselves alone and afraid. They gathered together to pray, and something remarkable happened: the Spirit of God came upon each of them, and they felt God with them, in a new and transformative way. This day of Pentecost is the day we set aside to celebrate that coming of the Holy Spirit to the disciples after Jesus' ascension into heaven; it was the beginning of the Christian church.

Originally a Jewish holiday known as *Shavu'ot* (which means "weeks" in Hebrew), Pentecost is a feast celebrating the grain harvest and marking the passage of seven weeks from Passover. "Pentecost" was its name in Greek, referring to the 50 days that pass in those seven weeks. Originally commanded by God of the Israelites in Leviticus 23, during the life of Christ Pentecost was celebrated by the Jewish people much as described in Deuteronomy 26, with farmers carrying baskets of wheat into Jerusalem and bringing them to the temple as a thank offering.[1] Grains were the earliest crops ready for harvest, and they offered to God the firstfruits of all He had given them.

Together with Passover and *Sukkot* (the harvest holiday in the fall), Pentecost was a pilgrimage festival where all the Jewish people were expected to make the journey to the temple in Jerusalem. This was a time for the community to be renewed as they all came into God's presence together. It was also a break from the everyday routine as they journeyed and celebrated together.

In the years before Jesus was born, rabbinical scholars studying Exodus 19 determined that the Torah was given on the day of *Shavu'ot*,

---

1 Dan Cohn-Sherbok, *Judaism: History, Belief and Practice* (New York, NY: Routledge, 2003), 509.

and so *Shavu'ot* also became associated with God giving the law to Moses on Mount Sinai after the exodus from Egypt. [2] For the Jewish people, this day when the law was given was one of the most important in all of human history. The law set them apart as God's people and gave them instructions for how to live. While the whole city of Jerusalem was celebrating God's gifts — from the provision of food to the protection of the law, and being set apart as God's holy people — it was appropriate timing for another gift to be given to the disciples.

Jesus had promised His disciples He would send them a Helper (see John 14:16–17, 26). So when they were alone and afraid after His ascension into heaven, they gathered to pray. Luke describes the scene for us in Acts 2:1–12:

> When the day of Pentecost arrived, they were all together in one place. And suddenly there came from heaven a sound like a mighty rushing wind, and it filled the entire house where they were sitting. And divided tongues as of fire appeared to them and rested on each one of them. And they were all filled with the Holy Spirit and began to speak in other tongues as the Spirit gave them utterance.
>
> Now there were dwelling in Jerusalem Jews, devout men from every nation under heaven. And at this sound the multitude came together, and they were bewildered, because each one was hearing them speak in his own language. And they were amazed and astonished, saying, "Are not all these who are speaking Galileans? And how is it that we hear, each of us in his own native language? Parthians and Medes and Elamites and residents of Mesopotamia, Judea and Cappadocia, Pontus and Asia, Phrygia and Pamphylia, Egypt and the parts of Libya belonging to Cyrene, and visitors from Rome, both Jews and proselytes, Cretans and Arabians—we hear them telling in our own tongues the mighty works of God." And all were amazed and perplexed, saying to one another, "What does this mean?"

The Holy Spirit miraculously gave the disciples the ability to speak to the crowds gathered in Jerusalem for the feast day in all their native languages. With the boldness of the Holy Spirit, Peter made the first public proclamation of the gospel, describing how Jesus defeated

---

2 Halperin, *The Faces of the Chariot* (Tuebingen, DE: Mohr Siebeck, 1998), 17–19.

death, rose again, and is seated at the right hand of God. The book of Acts records that, on the day of Pentecost, thousands of people believed and were baptized. Today, we can look back on Pentecost as the birth of the church in the New Testament, led by the Spirit of God and proclaiming the good news of Christ's redeeming love.

In the Old Testament, God's Spirit is often mentioned, starting in the second verse of Genesis chapter one! If the Holy Spirit was already at work on the earth, what changed at Pentecost? After the Day of Pentecost, the Holy Spirit remained with all believers, as a constant presence. In the new covenant, the Spirit has a more distinct, transforming power, remaking believers into the image of Christ (II Corinthians 3).

Moreover, Pentecost unites the church in a special way. It represents the reversal of the Tower of Babel,[3] where God had punished the people of earth for their pride and divided them by giving them different languages. The Holy Spirit enabled all the people to hear the message of the gospel on the day of Pentecost, no matter what their language or ethnicity. Through the Holy Spirit, God unites people from every language and community to be one body in faith.

Though Jesus charged His disciples to go and make disciples before His ascension, Pentecost marked the beginning of their public ministry preaching and teaching others and from that day and that place the gospel began to spread around the entire world. The first Pentecost was a turning point for the disciples and on the feast of Pentecost we remember that turning point, as well as the miracle of speaking in other tongues and the grace of having the Holy Spirit to lead and guide us today.

Pentecost is a season of both hope and mission. Jesus has given us the good news of the gospel and the help of the Holy Spirit, and He has promised to finish the work that He has begun. The church rejoices in her ability to participate in this work and remembers all of the blessings she has been given along the way.

Calendar

Pentecost takes place seven Sundays after Easter, so the date changes from year to year, reflecting the changes in the date of Easter. The date always falls during May or June.

---

3 Jaroslav Pelikan, *Acts* (Grand Rapids, MI: Brazos Press, 2005), 52.

The Traditions

Because of its origins as a Jewish holiday, Pentecost has been celebrated from the very first days of the church. It is mentioned in Acts 20:16 and I Corinthians 16:8, showing us its importance to the young church. From the early days of the church, connections have been made between the Torah being given to the Israelites on Pentecost and the Spirit being given to the disciples on Pentecost. Jerome, the translator of the Vulgate Bible, wrote, "There is Sinai, here Zion; there the trembling mountain, here the trembling house; there the flaming mountain, here the flaming tongues; there the noisy thunderings, here the sounds of many tongues; there the clangor of the ram's horn, here the notes of the gospel-trumpet."[4] The early church celebrated by prayer and sharing feasts together. It was a season of great joy as they remembered the gift of the Holy Spirit and how the gospel spread following Christ's ascension.

After Easter, Pentecost was one of the most common days for converts to be received into the church through baptism,[5] growing the church just as it grew on the Day of Pentecost in Acts. As the process for receiving new members developed, many traditions dressed converts in white robes for their baptism and reception into the church. Because of all the converts in white robes, Pentecost become known as "Whitsunday" in many parts of Europe, beginning in the Middle Ages. There are still churches that refer to Pentecost as Whitsunday.

In Moravian churches, Pentecost is typically marked with a love feast. Harkening back to the communal meals described in the New Testament (Acts 2:46), those who attend share a sweet bread or bun with coffee during a service of hymns and prayers.

The liturgical color for Pentecost is red in Western churches, to represent the flaming tongues of the Holy Spirit. For most traditions, it is the only red Sunday of the year. You will find many churches decorated with red flowers, red candles or even red balloons in addition to more traditional red paraments. To honor this unique day in the calendar, it has become customary in many churches for parishioners to wear red on Pentecost Sunday.

The main symbols for Pentecost are the dove to represent the Holy Spirit and the flame to represent the tongues of flame from the

---

4 *The International Standard Bible Encyclopædia* (Grand Rapids, MI: Eerdmans Publishing Co., 1995), 2319.
5 Tertullian, *On Baptism* (London, UK: SPCK, 1964), 19.

account of the day of Pentecost in Acts 2. In addition to the color red, many churches decorate with flames and doves for Pentecost Sunday.

New Traditions

Pentecost services can include Scripture readings in multiple languages. If churches speaking different languages share a facility, Pentecost is a great day to do a joint service together in the evening and celebrate how God is at work in both congregations. If this sort of service isn't possible in your area and you and your friends are not fluent in other languages, think of creative ways you can share in this experience. Perhaps you can use the internet to listen to Acts 2 in other languages; just use your favorite search engine to search for the audio.

One church in North Carolina has everyone dress in red, orange or yellow and gather for a group picture every Pentecost, reminding themselves of how they are to be aflame for the gospel in their community.

Have a birthday celebration for the church with friends or family. Make sure you serve a delicious birthday cake and cover it with lots of candles.

Do a study of the fruit or gifts of the Spirit in the New Testament in passages such as Romans 12, I Corinthians 12, and Galatians 5. These gifts include: love, joy, peace, patience, kindness, goodness, faithfulness, gentleness, self-control, serving, teaching, generosity, leadership, mercy, and wisdom. Spend time meditating on the characteristics God has been using the Holy Spirit to grow in your life and asking God to continue to make you more like Christ through the work of the Spirit. Write a few notes to other Christians with whom you are close, encouraging them by acknowledging ways you have seen the Holy Spirit growing these traits in them as well.

Make a bonfire or light sparklers to remind yourself of the flames and power of the Holy Spirit, which still remains with us today. Holding sparklers over their heads and pretending the tongues of fire are falling on them is particularly fun and engaging for children (take care to follow all safety precautions on the sparkler packaging).

Around the World

- In Denmark, Pentecost is often celebrated with Easter-like sunrise services on the beach. It is also traditional to hike and picnic on Pentecost.

- In Italy, rose petals are sometimes thrown from the balconies onto parishioners or scattered around the sanctuary to represent the descent of the tongues of fire, which gave Pentecost the nickname *Pascha Rosarum* — the Sunday (Passover) of Roses. Rose petals can also make great table decorations.
- From the Philippines to the United Kingdom, Pentecost has been a day churches organized parades of parishioners, wearing white or red, to encourage the joyful celebration of the day.
- In Poland, Russia, Ukraine and other Eastern European countries, homes are decorated with branches and flowers for Pentecost. The liturgical color for Pentecost is green in the Orthodox tradition and you will find Orthodox churches around the world decorated with green branches for Pentecost. The branches remind them of the evergreen, living church, which is always growing in grace and joy.

In the Kitchen

One of the most common dishes people share on Pentecost is a birthday cake, to celebrate the birthday of the church in the New Testament. You can decorate the cake with doves and cover it with lots of candles. It's appropriate to let everyone blow out the candles together!

Spicy foods such as chili, curry and cinnamon-spiced desserts can serve to remind of the tongues of fire that descended on the first disciples in the upper room.

As mentioned, Pentecost is often a day Moravian churches have a love feast. If you are unable to attend one in your area, here's a recipe for buns that is similar to the ones you might find at a love feast.

Moravian Lovefeast Buns

Ingredients
- *2 packages yeast*
- *½ cup warm water*
- *½ cup unsalted butter, softened*
- *1 cup sugar*
- *1 cup hot mashed potatoes, unseasoned*

- ½ cup milk
- 2 eggs, beaten
- ½ teaspoon nutmeg
- 2 tablespoons orange rind
- 2 tablespoons lemon rind
- 2 tablespoons orange juice
- 1 tablespoon fresh lemon juice
- 1½ pounds flour

Method

1. Combine the yeast and warm water, let sit about five minutes.
2. Cream together the butter and sugar.
3. Add the mashed potatoes, milk and beaten eggs; combine well.
3. Stir in the yeast and water mixture.
4. Mix spices together and add them.
5. Add flour gradually to make a soft, pliable dough.
6. Knead dough on a well-floured surface or with a dough hook until smooth.
7. Oil a large mixing bowl. Form the dough into a ball and set in the bowl.
8. Let the dough rise in a warm area, covered with a cloth, until it doubles in size (2–3 hours). Punch down and let rise again for 10 minutes.
9. Form the dough into small (3–4" diameter) balls with floured hands and place on a cookie sheet. Let them rise in a warm area, covered with a cloth, until doubled in size.
10. Preheat oven to 350° and bake until golden brown, about 15 to 20 minutes.

For the Very Young

The most important thing about sharing Pentecost with young children is helping them to understand the basic story. Reading the story in a story Bible such as Sally Lloyd-Jones's *Jesus Storybook Bible* can be immensely helpful. After children understand the basics of what happened on the day of Pentecost, help them to understand that the Spirit that came upon Jesus' disciples is the same Holy Spirit that is with us today, leading and helping us as we follow God.

Children retain material well through singing. After you have gone over the story of Pentecost, you can sing this to the tune of *"Frère Jacques"*

Holy Spirit, Holy Spirit
Promised one, promised one
Came with mighty wind, came with mighty wind and
Tongues of fire, tongues of fire.

Most of the creative ideas for celebrating Pentecost are very engaging to young children. They will more concretely understand Pentecost as the birthday of the church after they eat cake, or remember the symbolism of fire if Pentecost comes with an association of bonfires or sparklers.

Pentecost is a good springboard for family discussions about the work of the Holy Spirit in our hearts. After children are familiar with the story of Pentecost and that the Holy Spirit is with us, you can tell them about the fruit of the Spirit from Galatians 5. Explain that a tree can have good fruit or rotten fruit and that Christians want to have the good fruit of the Holy Spirit. There are several good songs about the fruit of the Spirit that you can learn together. Write down each fruit of the Spirit and brainstorm ways your family can show that fruit of the Spirit. Encourage your children by pointing out ways they already show the fruit of the Spirit.

Things to Make

Paper flames make fun decorations you can hang around any room for Pentecost. All that is required is construction paper, scissors and glue and even small children can participate. One church has a tradition of making flames during the Sunday school hour the week before and hanging them across the sanctuary overhead for Pentecost Sunday.

There are many ways to make doves to represent the Holy Spirit. You can use white card stock and coffee filters to make three-dimensional doves. First, cut a bird shape on the white card stock and then make a slit in the back. Fold the coffee filter up and slide it through the slit to be the wings. You can use a hole punch for an eye and an additional hole just before the wings so you can hang them up with yarn around the room or from light fixtures.

Since we celebrate the church on Pentecost, try making Pentecost-themed stained glass windows. To prepare, cut frames out of card stock. Then choose a shape to be the center of your window, such as a dove or a flame, and cut it out of black construction paper. Cut squares of tissue paper or cellophane in different colors to be the glass. Then use contact paper to put it all together. First set the contact paper down sticky side up, then the frame, then the shape. Fill all the space with the tissue paper and finish with another layer of contact paper. If you aren't going to hang them in a window, you can make a simpler collage of tissue paper squares on a piece of white paper and cover with your black construction paper symbol.

Beyond the Home

Pentecost is a good opportunity to do cross-cultural ministry as we remember how the Holy Spirit came and the gospel spread to people from different cultures and who spoke different languages. There are many ways you can participate in cross-cultural ministry without leaving the country, or even your neighborhood.

Invite an international student from a local college to your home for a meal and learn about their culture. If you don't know any personally, many campuses have para-church ministries geared towards international students and they are always looking for new people to partner with them.

Find a free class for English language learners in your area and ask what you can do to support their ministry, such as bringing a snack or providing childcare. This can be a simple way to get to know immigrants living in your area.

Call a local office that settles refuges (such as Church World Service, International Rescue Committee, and Lutheran Immigration and Refuge Services) and see what opportunities you have to serve newcomers or donate supplies. You can even organize a drive at your church for whatever is most needed.

If your church is doing vacation Bible school or backyard Bible clubs over the summer, find a way to include children of immigrants in your programs, particularly by providing transportation. Use the contacts you have made to personally invite them to participate with you.

Pray for any missionaries around the world that you and/or your church supports. Invite a missionary on furlough who is gathering funds or prayer partners to share with your church or small group about their ministry. Pentecost can be a great opportunity to share with children about how the gospel is still being spread around the world.

Write an encouraging letter to a missionary you support and send a care package with treats from home or things they need.

Resources

Seasonal Scripture Readings

Acts 2
Ezekiel 37:1–14
I Corinthians 12:3–13

Suggestions for Memorization:

But the Helper, the Holy Spirit, whom the Father will send in my name, he will teach you all things and bring to your remembrance all that I have said to you. Peace I leave with you; my peace I give to you. Not as the world gives do I give to you. Let not your hearts be troubled, neither let them be afraid. — John 14:26–27

And Peter said to them, "Repent and be baptized every one of you in the name of Jesus Christ for the forgiveness of your sins, and you will receive the gift of the Holy Spirit. For the promise is for you and for your children and for all who are far off, everyone whom the Lord our God calls to himself." — Acts 2:38–39

The fruit of the Spirit is love, joy, peace, patience, kindness, goodness, faithfulness, gentleness, self-control; against such things there is no law. — Galatians 5:22–23

Songs of the Season

"Come Down, O Love Divine," *Bianco da Siena*, tr. Richard Frederick Littledale.
"Come Holy Ghost, Creator Blest," *Rhabanus Maurus*, tr. Edward

Caswall.

"Come, Holy Ghost, God and Lord," Martin Luther, tr. Catherine Winkworth.

"Spirit of God, Descend Upon My Heart," George Croly.

"The Fruit," by Seeds Family Worship.

"The Fruit of the Spirit's Not A Coconut," by Brentwood Kids.

Seasonal Reading

For Children
The Very First Christians, by Paul Maier.

For All Ages
"Whitsunday," by George Herbert.
"Whitsunday," by John Keble.
"Whitsun Day," by Christina Rossetti.

For More Serious Reading
Renovation of the Heart, by Dallas Willard.
The Deep Things of God, by Fred Sanders.

Prayers

Table Blessing

Bless, O Lord, this day of Pentecost and this meal we are about to receive. Use this food to strengthen us and remind us of the good gifts You have provided, even Your Holy Spirit. Just as You showed Ezekiel in days of old, breathe life into our dry bones and bring us new life through your Spirit. Use that Spirit to guide, sustain and comfort us as we walk in Your ways. Amen.

Bedtime Prayer

Triune God, we are thankful for Your Holy Spirit that abides with us through our days and nights. Christ promised the Holy Spirit would come as a comforter to His followers when He was no longer with them, and we pray that by that same Spirit we would be given comfort and rest tonight. Even as we sleep, renew us with Your Holy Spirit so that like Your disciples on the day of Pentecost, we might proclaim the good news of the gospel with boldness as we walk with grace and truth. In the name of the Father, the Son and the Holy Spirit, Amen.

A Collect

Almighty God, on this day you opened the way of eternal life to every race and nation by the promised gift of your Holy Spirit. Shed abroad this gift throughout the world by the preaching of the Gospel, that it may reach to the ends of the earth; through Jesus Christ our Lord, who lives and reigns with you, in the unity of the Holy Spirit, one God, for ever and ever. Amen.[6]

6 *Book of Common Prayer* (1986), 227.

Ordinary Time

by Ann E. Dominguez

Introduction to Ordinary Time

The church year moves through two similar cycles of repentance, celebration, and life in a new reality. The year begins with Advent, a season for self-examination and repentance to prepare us for Christmas (the celebration). During Epiphany, we take to the world what we have learned of an eternal God who would step into time. Likewise, we spend Lent in repentance and examination, then experience the joy of Easter and an ordination at Pentecost. Finally, we have the season of Ordinary Time to practice living in the reality of the resurrection. The parallels between these two sequences are so strong that some traditions consider Ordinary Time to be two seasons: the first falling between Epiphany Sunday and Ash Wednesday, and the second from Pentecost to Advent. Ordinary Time is the longest season of the church year, encompassing most of the summer and autumn, yet most of us have no sense of what this season contributes to our celebration of time as holy — as ordained.

Ordinary Time is a season bookmarked by feasts. We begin the season with Trinity Sunday, celebrating the unity of the Godhead, and finish with the celebrations of All Saints', Thanksgiving[1] and Christ the King. All Saints' is the time we recognize and honor those who have gone before us — those who have run the race set out for them. On Pentecost, both they and we were ordained to live a life for Christ, and on All Saints', we celebrate those who have done it. Christ the King celebrates the glory of the King, the entire point of creation. Thus Ordinary Time is the culmination of the church year, when we bear fruit and there is a harvest for the King.

The challenge of Ordinary Time is that it doesn't feel important. It can be difficult to sustain a sense of time as holy through the forty

---

1 In Canada, the order is Thanksgiving, All Saints', Christ the King.

days of Lent, or even the twelve days of Christmas. And yet we need a season when the decorations are taken down and the work of living is done. The dictionary definition of "ordinary" is "normal": without special or distinctive features. Uninteresting. Commonplace. Ordinal numbers are those which describe what we are counting: the first, second, or third week since Pentecost. Our lives are described in many ways by counting: one's 30th birthday, referencing birth as the transformative event. The year 2014 is the 2014th year since Christ's birth, the event that transformed the world. The 22nd week of Ordinary Time is the 22nd Sunday since the church was transformed at Pentecost.

In church definitions, the "ordinary" are those parts of the mass or service that do not vary from day to day. The 1969 Second Vatican Council coined the term "Ordinary Time," referring to the numbered weeks between Pentecost and Advent. The adjectival form of "ordinary" comes from the Latin word for "orderly." It is *how* we live our ordinary, daily lives that shows our true characters. Thus it is our living of Ordinary Time that defines who we are.

The biblical model of time-keeping, building from days and seasons to years, contrasts with our culture's approach to breaking days into hours, hours into minutes and minutes into seconds. The clock can be a harsh taskmaster if we don't have a sense of time as holy. The liturgy of the hours and the seasons of the church year help to refocus our eyes on the holiness of time.

The John 21 account of Jesus' and the disciples' breakfast on the beach is a perfect illustration of what Ordinary Time is to be. It was after the resurrection but before Pentecost. The disciples had already glimpsed the risen Christ but couldn't spend days and nights by His side, peppering Him with questions as they used to. They had not yet been commissioned for their new work; exhausted with grief and uncertain how to proceed with life, the disciples returned to what they knew before Jesus. They took the boat out to fish, but they caught nothing. Had they forgotten what their lives were like before Jesus and how to practice their profession according to the world's rules? Or did their nets remain empty because the very nature of the world had been changed by the resurrection?

Jesus, unrecognized on the beach next to His breakfast barbecue, called to them to cast their net on the *other* side of the boat. John immediately recognized Jesus, who loved him. But it was Peter — impetuous Peter, who said and did exactly the wrong thing with his knowledge and therefore was the one most like us — who jumped out of the boat and swam to shore to fall at Jesus' feet.

Not only was their net nearly too full to haul in, but Jesus had made them breakfast: the most important, and most ordinary, meal of the day. It was here, on the beach after a hard night's work, that Jesus met them, His disciples. He fed them. He reinstated Peter by commanding him three times, once for each of Peter's denials, to feed His sheep as a sign of his love for Jesus. Was it this experience that inspired Peter's beautiful words from I Peter 1:3: "Blessed be the God and Father of our Lord Jesus Christ! According to his great mercy, he has caused us to be born again to a living hope through the resurrection of Jesus Christ from the dead"?

And so here is our model for Ordinary Time. We are to go about our ordained but ordinary work, whether that be washing clothes or fishing or doing other people's taxes.[2] We are to remain attentive, listening for the voice of Jesus telling us to do our work in a different way: a way informed by our knowledge of who He is. And we are to fall at His feet in worship, ready to be fed day by day and to feed His sheep.

Thus Ordinary Time is our chance to be whole people — integrated people, for whom Christmas and Easter are not isolated holidays, but life-changing events that have transformed the very fabric of the world and our experience in it. We are to become people in whom the Living God grows and breathes and inspires work which brings Him glory. Ordinary Time is the season in which we become saints by the daily, unchanging disciplines of confession, repentance, forgiveness, celebration, and service, that our lives would reflect the glory of Christ the King.

Calendar

Ordinary Time begins the Monday after Pentecost and ends the Saturday before Advent. Its feasts include Trinity Sunday (the Sunday after Pentecost), the Transfiguration (the Sunday closest to August 6),[3] All Saints' Sunday (the first Sunday of November), Thanksgiving, and

---

2 In a day when books and pastors brow-beat Christians about not living their lives radically enough, Ordinary Time affirms that the everyday work and pastimes are godly and right. Those interested in this culturally contradictory message of Ordinary Time might find Matt Redmond's book, *The God Of The Mundane: Reflections on Ordinary Life for Ordinary Christians*, a worthwhile read.

3 In some traditions, the Transfiguration is celebrated on the Sunday before Ash Wednesday. See the companion chapter on Epiphany and Lent for more information.

Christ the King Sunday (the last Sunday before Advent). Ordinary Time can last as long as 27 weeks. In some traditions, Ordinary Time can be 33 to 34 weeks as it includes the weeks between Epiphany and Ash Wednesday.

The lectionary readings and collects (prayers) for Ordinary Time are numbered 1 through 33 and are known as Propers. The 33 or 34 weeks of Propers and readings in the Catholic and Anglican liturgies are split between the season between Epiphany and Lent (*Epiphany* or *Ordinary Time I*); and the season between Pentecost and Advent (known as *Ordinary Time II*). The distribution of weeks between the two seasons varies from year to year. Thus, Propers 1 through 5 (or 6, 7, 8, or 9 depending on the date of Ash Wednesday) are used before Lent. The Monday after Pentecost, we begin with Proper 6 (or 7, 8, or 9) and conclude the season with Proper 33 or 34 on Christ the King Sunday.

Some Protestant traditions (especially the Methodist and some Presbyterian churches) split this second, longer portion of Ordinary Time into two parts: Pentecost during the summer (ending the last Sunday of August), and Dominiontide or Kingdomtide (ending with Christ the King Sunday). The name Kingdomtide is also used by the Church of England to designate the sub-season from All Saints' Sunday until Christ the King Sunday.

Some lectionaries will mark the Sundays of Ordinary Time in relation to Trinity Sunday (the first Sunday after Pentecost Sunday), which is technically the first Sunday of Ordinary Time. Thus the weeks may be called "Trinity Sunday," "First Sunday after Trinity," etc.

Traditions

The ecclesiastical color for Ordinary Time is green. Green symbolizes growth and the hope of new life, brought by the resurrection.

Trinity Sunday

Trinity Sunday, celebrated the first Sunday after Pentecost, celebrates the Triune nature of God. Its color is white, and many churches celebrate it by reading aloud the Creed of Athanasius, which is one of the first accepted articulations of the doctrine of the Trinity. If your church does not read it during the service, reading it yourself or with your family might add to your understanding and celebration of this day. Traditional readings are Matthew 28:19; II Corinthians 13:14; John 1:18; John 15:26. J.S. Bach composed at least three cantatas for Trinity

Sunday (BWV 165, 176, and 129) which are often performed as a part of a Trinity Sunday celebration.

Transfiguration

Transfiguration Sunday, celebrated on August 6, is a major feast of Ordinary Time. We change the church paraments and vestments to white, which symbolize the shining garments Jesus wore as He was transfigured into His glorious state before the eyes of the disciples. Filling the church and the home with light is a fitting way to celebrate this holy day.

In Mark 8, we see Jesus as He fed the 4,000, taught the disciples, and healed the blind. Peter confessed Jesus as the Christ, and then Jesus predicted His death. Peter pulled Jesus aside and scolded Him for speaking this way. "But turning and seeing his disciples, he rebuked Peter and said, 'Get behind me, Satan! For you are not setting your mind on the things of God, but on the things of man.'" (Mark 8:33). How true this is of us: we can watch Jesus feeding the hungry, read His words of teaching and be healed, but we still have our minds on earthly things. And how kind was Jesus that in Mark 9, immediately following His rebuke of Peter, He brought Peter with James and John up onto the mountain to see His Transfiguration (Mark 9:2–13).

In the Transfiguration passage, Jesus conferred with Moses and Elijah. This event prefigured the tearing of the veil between heaven and earth. Likewise, we have a foretaste of the glory that was and is to come, and that already exists in the heavenly realm. Again, here we have a glimpse of the eternal that somehow continues all around us mortals who are trapped in linear time. No wonder Peter wanted to stay on that mountaintop!

And yet Jesus led them back down toward Jerusalem and His march to the cross. For this reason, some churches choose to celebrate Transfiguration during the season of Epiphany, seeing it as a step toward the cross. The Catholic and Anglican traditions celebrate Transfiguration on the Sunday closest to August 6, where it punctuates the long green season of Ordinary Time. We see the glory of Christ, but we have to come back down the mountain to live our ordinary days. The reminder that we, like Moses and Elijah, are in eternal communion with Jesus foreshadows All Saints' and reminds us of the goal of our own daily work and lives: to celebrate the glory of Jesus.

Reformation Day

Reformation Day, celebrated on the Sunday before All Saints', commemorates Martin Luther's nailing of his 95 Theses on the door of the Castle Church in Wittenberg on October 31, 1517. But more than celebrating Luther's specific act, Reformation Day recognizes the Reformation's commitment to the preservation of truth and orthodoxy.

Some Presbyterian churches celebrate by having bagpipes and traditional Scottish music played in their service. Including one or more of Martin Luther's hymns (the most famous being "A Mighty Fortress is Our God") in the service or a celebration in a home would be appropriate. Likewise, a special offering toward a ministry focused on translating the Bible into the language of an unreached people group would be a fitting way to celebrate the Reformation's emphasis on each believer's having full access to the Word of God in his or her own language.

All Saints'

All Saints' is celebrated on November 1. Some dated feasts are celebrated in the church either the Sunday before or after the date, but All Saints' is always celebrated on November 1 and the Sunday *after* November 1. The liturgical color for this holy day is white, reminding us of the white raiment promised us in Revelation.

We are celebrating those who have gone before us and who are even at this moment at the feet of Jesus. This celebration often acquires a special meaning for those who have lost loved ones in the previous year, and many churches will give special recognition to those saints from their own congregations who have died. Likewise, in a family this day can be an opportunity to celebrate loved ones who have died. Whether or not you celebrate individual saints recognized by the church, All Saints' Sunday is the perfect time to celebrate the spiritual parents, brothers and sisters whom God used to bring us into His family.

We are at the end of the church year by All Saints', and the temptation to lose heart is strong at this time of year. The world encourages us to be looking ahead to Christmas already (never mind Advent!) with songs about Santa and the countdown of shopping days left all around us. Instead, we are reminded not to give up on walking the quiet, daily walk we've been assigned. Pausing to acknowledge the cloud of witnesses is necessary to remind us that our ultimate goal is not located in Christmas, but in a life that reflects the resurrection.

Thanksgiving

While Thanksgiving is celebrated as a secular holiday, the command to give thanks runs throughout all of Scripture. Recognizing that it is God's hand that gives us all gifts makes this holiday a holy day. Again we see the emphasis on food. Truly, do we think of that word feast apart from food? The traditional foods of Thanksgiving are autumnal harvest foods. In our modern age, in which almost any food can be had for a price at any time of year, we are disconnected from the natural rhythm that made Thanksgiving an autumnal holiday. But our regard for the foods of the season will connect us to the rhythm of the church year.

Christ the King

This feast falls on the last Sunday before Advent and is the feast that wraps up Ordinary Time. It is often lost as we plow ahead toward Christmas, but it is a celebration of Christ's glory and a foretaste of the eternal reality. On Christ the King Sunday, we celebrate Christ's supremacy over creation. We serve a mighty, glorious King, and celebrating Him in all His glory puts into focus the shocking humility with which He took on flesh at Christmas. This celebration also looks forward to Christ's second coming as Judge. The liturgical color is white and serves as a punctuation mark between the green of Ordinary Time and the purple of Advent.

New Traditions

During Ordinary Time, the lectionary passages concentrate on the mission of the church (reflecting Pentecost) and the dominion of Christ over the world. But unlike the penitential seasons of Advent and Lent, and the celebratory seasons of Christmas and Easter, there are few traditional practices that are unique to Ordinary Time. Instead, Ordinary Time is an opportunity to reflect on how our daily lives further Christ's kingdom, both in personal discipline and corporate practice.

Pentecost was an amazing moment in history when the third person of the Trinity descended on the entire church at a specific time. This act of the Holy Spirit parallels the incarnation that happened at Christmas. Pentecost happened for a reason: to further the gospel's spread through the world. Acts 2:43–47 gives us further specifics about how the gift of the Spirit was embodied in the church:

> And awe came upon every soul, and many wonders and signs were being done through the apostles. And all who believed were together and had all things in common. And they were

selling their possessions and belongings and distributing the proceeds to all, as any had need. And day by day, attending the temple together and breaking bread in their homes, they received their food with glad and generous hearts, praising God and having favor with all the people. And the Lord added to their number day by day those who were being saved.

This response to the Holy Spirit is a model for our daily, ordinary lives. The church practiced the corporate habits of teaching/learning, fellowship within the church, breaking bread together, and corporate prayer. These, together with giving to anyone who had need and praising God, bore the fruit of a harvest of souls.

Sacrifices

Daily sacrifices might include forgoing your coffee habit to give that money to the church to feed the hungry. Perhaps you will be led to eat meat once less per week in order to support your church's food pantry. Or maybe you will give up a night of TV each week to participate in a tutoring program at a prison or in a ministry for the homeless. Perhaps your family will minister once a month at a shelter, or you will be led to give one day's salary per month to the church's mission fund. Maybe you will tithe out of your clothing budget to provide school uniforms for children in Africa.

Ordinary Time affords us the luxury of habit. Perhaps you desire to cultivate a fruit of the Spirit. Maybe you have prayerfully discerned a need to practice a specific discipline. Ordinary Time is long enough that your growth in this area does not have to be a sprint but can be a marathon (or a slow and steady walk). There is time to memorize an epistle, or copy a gospel verse by verse, or to read the entire New Testament. This long green season is truly long enough to plant a seed, cultivate the plant, and reap a harvest for Christ.

Jesus's thrice-asked question to Peter on the beach, "Simon, son of John, do you love me?" was answered thus: "Feed my sheep." Clearly

Peter, as an apostle, had a very specific task ahead of him as he went to fulfill this command. But Peter as a prototype for us, the ordinary disciples, already had received Jesus' description of what that meant, as described in Matthew 25:35–37. Jesus painted a picture of the loving response we should be offering Him: to feed the hungry, give drink to the thirsty, invite the stranger in, clothe the naked, minister to the sick, and visit the imprisoned. What we began as an act of Christmas charity or a Lenten sacrifice can grow roots in us during Ordinary Time. Ask the Holy Spirit to show you how daily, weekly, and monthly sacrifices can be used to bring Christ's Kingdom here on earth.

Likewise, the early church's model of eating together regularly may inspire a corporate celebration in your church. Many families choose to begin their celebration of Sabbath with a dinner that is reminiscent of the Jewish tradition of Shabbat, the meal which begins the Jewish Sabbath. Traditionally a Shabbat supper is marked by the lighting of special candles, the reading of Scripture, and an elaborate, leisurely meal. Some churches host a weekly Sabbath meal which welcomes guests and strangers. A Saturday night Sabbath meal in your home might be a place to invite your neighbors, or a time to plant a special tradition of welcoming God's rest into the rhythm of your week.

The end of the church year is also a great time to plan ahead by planting bulbs or a spring-blooming bush like forsythia that will bloom at Easter.

Around the World

An Irish tradition associated with Ordinary Time is the making of a bonfire on the eve of the Feast of St. John the Baptist (June 24). The bonfire, often fueled with all the "old" that people were getting rid of, is a symbol of the ending of the old as the New Covenant of Christ begins. Ordinary Time usually begins in summer and ends in late autumn. The nights grow longer and the darkness around us deepens as we march on from the resurrection, and yet we are called to keep the flame of Pentecost alive even in the world's darkness. A bonfire is a great reminder of the light and the heat of the Holy Spirit.

Without the major feasts such as Christmas and Easter to mark our days, Ordinary Time celebrates the week in a way the rest of the year cannot. We begin our week with Sabbath rest, which gives us the strength for our work in its various forms. The Jewish tradition of Sabbath keeping can offer much toward our experience of Ordinary Time.

Making a Sabbath means consciously planning 24 hours (whether from sundown Saturday night to sundown Sunday, or Sunday morning to Monday morning) in which we set aside the world's demands in order to focus on God and "heavenly things." For those pastors and public servants who have no choice but to work on Sunday, their day of rest can come during the week, perhaps by not shopping or watching television during this time, seeking a midweek church service, or spending this day with family.

In the Kitchen

These are days for simple food. Staples that nourish both in the making and in the eating. Homemade bread — once a week, or once a day. Yogurt poured over berries. The practice of gardening, whether you have two pots on a windowsill or an acre (or more), draws us into God's own design: earth created and redeemed, producing fruit in season. In the northern hemisphere, Ordinary Time encompasses the season in which seeds are planted, watered, and harvested. The beauty of that cycle can inform how we see our food. In June, berries and greens are plentiful. In July, potatoes and zucchini are often denigrated as common foods, and yet their very abundance reflects God's bounty. Taking the time to enjoy a ripe tomato in August, as opposed to one forced out of season, puts us in tune with the garden God planted. Receiving our food as a gift from the hand of God is counter-cultural and can be a sign of a post-resurrection people.

The Mennonite tradition has much to say about the simplicity and importance of food: how our respect for growing the food and feeding our bodies reflects our respect for God. The cookbook *Simply in Season* has a wealth of reflections on food culture within a Christian context, and it is rich in wisdom as well as in excellent recipes.

In these days of TVs in every room and a million diversions at our fingertips, our society has lost its connection with food. We buy high-calorie "convenience food" to eat at home and then drive to the gym to work it off. Ordinary Time offers us the opposite: time to incorporate the slow joys of planting, tending, harvesting and preparing our food. It is not a time of major feasts or fasts. Instead, we are invited to make all time sacred: the preparing of a meal as much as the eating of it.

For the Very Young

Children thrive on ordinary celebrations. The world's celebration of great feasts of Easter and Christmas can lead to frenzied anticipation that often obscure the meaning of the holy days, as well as Advent and Lent that precede them. The traditions of gift-giving associated with these holy days can be all that a small child remembers. But a modest, small, weekly celebration, such as a Sabbath dinner, can be just right for pointing a young child toward God.

The Jewish Sabbath begins on Saturday night with a special meal which can be made special by the best dishes and a tablecloth, a special prayer, or dessert. It is an ideal time to bless each child, or remember one's baptism anniversary. A Sabbath meal is a good time to welcome friends to your table. Children enjoy decorating the table with flowers from the garden or candles. They might choose a prayer from a book of prayers. Reading the week's gospel reading gives it a night to soak into us before the service the next morning. Setting apart Saturday night for this simple celebration assures that we are all rested and focused before our church celebration on Sunday.

Thanksgiving offers many creative ways to model counting our blessings. A family can wrap a shoebox with paper and cut a slot in the lid. This can be kept out during the year for dropping thanksgivings into, and then opened at Thanksgiving to read each gift aloud. A Thanksgiving journal, in which each family members records gifts they received from God during the year, can be read at Thanksgiving as well. Or thank offerings can be written on "leaves" of paper and hung on a paper tree on the wall. Any way you choose to record God's faithfulness to you will serve.

For Christ the King Sunday, the crown is versatile symbol for a children's celebration. It can be emblazoned on a cupcake, made into an ornament for the Christmas tree, or made in paper form to wear.

Things to Make

The daily rhythms of Ordinary Time invite us to live in the present. Each moment is sacred: an act of faithfulness with the time we have been given. Children may enjoy using cloth napkins they have sewn, and a handmade dishcloth adds an element of beauty to a mundane task. Whether by knitting, sewing or crafting a wooden table, incorporating the beauty of handmade art into daily life reminds us of the holiness of each day.

Whatever form of beauty most speaks to you, offer it each day to God. Whether you are playing or listening to a piece of music or putting flowers on the table for a meal, offer it to God. Thank Him for it, and for allowing you to perceive it today. Enjoy the majesty of the mountains towering above us, or the shine of the sun on water, or the weeds blooming in the sidewalk cracks, and offer your thanks to God for what He has made.

Beyond the Home

The Lutheran tradition of a "Hunger Meal" is especially appropriate to Ordinary Time. The idea is to share a community meal that makes us aware of hunger in the world. Unlike a fast in which everyone foregoes a meal to give the money to be spent on feeding the hungry, a hunger meal causes us to see the inequality in food distribution around the world. Thus, everyone contributes (usually equally) toward the meal, but the food is distributed unequally, in proportion to the pattern of the world. Fifteen percent are served a gourmet, several-course meal. Twenty-five percent receive a simple meal of rice and vegetables. The remaining guests, 60 percent of them, receive only a small bowl of rice. Follow the meal with a worship service which allows time to reflect on the "justice" of the world and the mercy of God. On its own, this Hunger Meal is a powerful example of the brokenness of the world. Following this meal in a week or a month with a Jubilee Meal, in which everyone receives an abundance, shows the sharp contrast between the ways of the world and the ways of God.

Traditionally Thanksgiving is an opportunity to welcome the stranger into our homes. Some churches celebrate Thanksgiving by providing baskets of food (everything needed for a Thanksgiving dinner) to needy families in their area. Other churches welcome the needy of the community to a feast in the church, which families within the church share.

Resources

Seasonal Scripture Readings

This season is long enough to choose one of the gospels and dive deeply into it, reading it through once a month to let the mysteries of Jesus in all aspects soak into you. Try reading the Psalms of Ascent (Psalms 120–134); the Sermon on the Mount (Matthew 5–7 or Luke 6:17–49); John 21; Matthew 25:31–46. Or read through the epistles, allowing the Word to transform your daily living.

For Christ the King, *The Revised Common Lectionary* in the Book of Common Prayer suggests reading Jeremiah 23:1–6, Luke 1:68 79, and Colossians 1:11–20, all passages which address Christ's kingship.

Suggestions for Memorization:

For Ordinary Time:

Blessed be the God and Father of our Lord Jesus Christ! According to his great mercy, he has caused us to be born again to a living hope through the resurrection of Jesus Christ from the dead. — I Peter 1:3

Seeing the crowds, he went up on the mountain, and when he sat down, his disciples came to him. And he opened his mouth and taught them, saying: "Blessed are the poor in spirit, for theirs is the kingdom of heaven. Blessed are those who mourn, for they shall be comforted. Blessed are the meek, for they shall inherit the earth. Blessed are those who hunger and thirst for righteousness, for they shall be satisfied. Blessed are the merciful, for they shall receive mercy. Blessed are the pure in heart, for they shall see God. Blessed are the peacemakers, for they shall be called sons of God. Blessed are those who are persecuted for righteousness' sake, for theirs is the kingdom of heaven. Blessed are you when others revile you and persecute you and utter all kinds of evil against you falsely on my account. Rejoice and be glad, for your reward is great in heaven, for so they persecuted the prophets who were before you." — Matthew 5:1–13

For All Saints':

Therefore, since we are surrounded by so great a cloud of witnesses, let us also lay aside every weight, and sin which clings so closely, and let us run with endurance the race that is set before us, looking to Jesus, the founder and perfecter of our faith, who for the joy that was set before him endured the cross, despising the shame, and is seated at the right hand of the throne of God. — Hebrews 12:1–3

For Thanksgiving:

Then he appointed some of the Levites as ministers before the ark of the Lord, to invoke, to thank, and to praise the Lord, the God of Israel — I Chronicles 16:4

…give thanks in all circumstances; for this is the will of God in Christ Jesus for you. — I Thessalonians 4:18

Any or all of Psalm 136 would be appropriate for Thanksgiving.

Seasonal Songs

This season is a great time to meditate on the music of the church, spending a few weeks on selected songs sung in worship, allowing the words to sink into us. For children, knowing the music allows them to participate more fully in worship. The Doxology is perfect as an Ordinary Time grace before meals.

For Trinity Sunday:
"*O heilges Geist- und Wasserbad, BWV 165*," J.S. Bach.
"*Es ist ein trotzig und verzagt Ding, BWV 176*," J.S. Bach.
"*Gelobet sei der Herr, mein Gott, BWV 129*," J.S. Bach.
"Father, we praise you," Gregory the Great, trans. Percy Dearmer.

For Transfiguration:
"We have come at Christ's own bidding," Carl P. Daw.
"How good Lord to be here/Tis Good Lord to Be Here," Robinson.
"Christ, upon the mountain peak," Brian Wren.
"Lord, it is good for us to be," Arthur Penrhyn Stanley.
"Transfigured Christ, none comprehends," Alan Gaunt.
"Shine, Jesus, Shine," Graham Kendrick.
"Fairest Lord Jesus," trans. Joseph A. Seiss.
"A Face that Shone," Michael Card.

For Reformation Day:
"A Mighty Fortress is Our God," Martin Luther.
"The Church's One Foundation," Samuel John Stone.

For All Saints':
"For All the Saints," William How.
"I Sing a Song of the Saints of God," Lesbia Scott.

For Thanksgiving:
"Now Thank We All Our God," Martin Rinkart, trans. Catherine Winkworth.
"We Gather Together," *Nederlandtsch Gedencklanck*, trans. Theodore Baker.
"Nothing Compares," Third Day.
"Life of Praise," Casting Crowns.
"Indescribable," Chris Tomlin.

For Christ the King:
"Crown Him with Many Crowns," Matthew Bridges and Godfrey Thring.
"Hail to the King," Larry Hampton.
"All Hail the Power of Jesus' Name," Edward Perronet.
"*Te Deum*"/"Holy God, we praise thy name," trans. Clarance A. Walworth.
"The Man Comes Around," Johnny Cash.

Seasonal Books

For Children
The Lord's Prayer, Psalm 23, by Tim Ladwig.
Pilgrim's Progress, adapted by Gary D. Schmidt and illustrated by Barry Moser.
The Last Battle, by C.S. Lewis (For Christ the King Sunday).

For Everyone:
At the Still Point: A Literary Guide to Prayer in Ordinary Time, by Sarah Arthur.
A Timbered Choir: The Sabbath Poems 1979–1997, by Wendell Berry.
The Freedom of Simplicity, by Richard Foster.
The Kingdom of Ordinary Time: Poems, by Marie Howe.
The World's Last Night by C.S. Lewis (For Christ the King Sunday).

Simply In Season, Mary Beth Lind.
Living More with Less, by Doris Janzen Longacre.
One Thousand Gifts, by Ann Voskamp.
Mudhouse Sabbath, by Lauren Winner.

For More Serious Reading:
The Spiritual Discipline Handbook, Adele Ahlberg Calhoun.
Celebration of Discipline, by Richard Foster.
Hearing God, by Dallas Willard.
The God of the Mundane: Reflections on Ordinary Life for Ordinary Christians, by Matt Redmond.

Prayers

The Psalms — 150 of them — offer us a wealth of prayer. Ordinary Time, lasting 180 to 230 days, gives us ample time to pray through the Psalms. Or, for a deeper look at the riches in the Psalms, you could choose the Psalms of Ascent (Psalms 120–134) and focus on each one for one to three weeks at a time.

Collects For Ordinary Time:

O Lord, who created the universe and called time holy, we pray for Your grace to live this ordinary day as sacred. In Your mercy, enable us to hold Your gifts in the palms of our hands and see in them Your blessings. In Your name we pray, Amen.

- or this -

O Lord, who stepped from Eternity into time, grant that we may find a window to Eternity in the minutes ordained to us this day. May we, as beings created in Your image, be able to look back at the work we did today and say, "It is good." In Your name, Amen.

For Transfiguration Sunday:

Lord Jesus, You who were glorified by God on the mountaintop, grant us grace to catch a glimpse of Your eternal glory before us every day. May we, transformed by Your presence, join in praise of Your wonderful majesty with Your prophets and servants who have gone before. Amen.

For All Saints' Sunday:

Almighty God, you have knit together your elect in one communion and fellowship in the mystical body of your Son Christ our Lord: Give us grace so to follow your blessed saints in all virtuous and godly living, that we may come to those ineffable joys that you have prepared for those who truly love you; through Jesus Christ our Lord, who with you and the Holy Spirit lives and reigns, one God, in glory everlasting. Amen.[4]

For Thanksgiving:

Almighty and gracious Father, we give you thanks for the fruits of the earth in their season and for the labors of those who harvest them. Make us, we pray, faithful stewards of your great bounty, for the provision of our necessities and the relief of all who are in need, to the glory of your Name; through Jesus Christ our Lord, who lives and reigns with you and the Holy Spirit, one God, now and for ever. Amen.[5]

For Christ the King:

Christ our King, image of the invisible God and firstborn over all creation, we praise You. In Your mercy, You have reconciled to Yourself all things, whether things on earth or things in heaven, by making peace through Your blood shed on the cross. Thank You for giving us a place in Your eternal kingdom. Grant that we may serve You now and all our days, with joy and faith in Your supremacy over all the temporary authorities and powers here on earth. Amen.

Any of the Creeds serve well as prayers for Christ the King, as does meditation on the great mystery: "Christ has died, Christ is risen, Christ will come again."

---

4 *Book of Common Prayer* (1986), 245.
5 Ibid., 246.

Works Cited

Adam, Adolf. *The Liturgical Year: its history and its meaning after the reform of the liturgy.* Trans. Matthew J. O'Connell. New York: Pueblo Publishing Company, 1981.

A Manual of Eastern Orthodox Prayers. Crestwood, NY: St. Vladimir's Seminary Press: 1983.

Augustine of Hippo. *On Christian Teaching,* trans. R.P.H. Green. Oxford University Press, USA, 2008

Bede (the Venerable). *Ecclesiastical History of the English People.,* trans. J.A. Giles. London: George Bell & Sons, 1903.

The Book of Common Prayer. New York: Church Publishing Incorporated, 1986.

The Book of Common Prayer. 1928.

Chrysostom, Saint John. *Sermon on the Statutes.*

Cohn-Sherbok, Dan. *Judaism: History, Belief and Practice.* London: Routledge, 2003.

Collins, Ace. *Stories Behind the Great Traditions of Christmas.* Grand Rapids: Zondervan, 2003.

Egeria's Travels. John Wilkinson, trans. Oxford: Aris & Phillips, 1999.

Elliott, Msgr. Peter. *Ceremonies of the Liturgical Year According to the Modern Roman Rite.* Ignatius Press, 2002.

Eliot, T. S. "Ash Wednesday", *Collected Poems 1909-1962.* New York: Harcourt Brace & Company, 1963.

Ganns, George E., ed. *Ignatius of Loyola, Spiritual Exercises and Other Works,* Classics of Western Spirituality. Mahwah, NJ: Paulist Press, 1991.

Gross, Bobby. *Living the Christian Year: Time to Inhabit the Story of*

God. Downers Grove: InterVarsity Press, 2009.

Gulevich, Tanya. *Christmas from A to Z.* Chicago: KWS Publishers: 2011.

Halperin, David J. *Faces of the Chariot.* Tübingen: Coronet Books, 1988.

The Holy Bible, English Standard Version. Crossway Bibles, 2001.

The Holy Bible, New International Version. Biblica: 2011.

Hopkins, Gerard M. *Poems and Prose.* London: Penguin Books, 1985.

The Hymnal 1982. New York: Church Publishing Incorporated, 1985.

The International Standard Bible Encyclopaedia, s.v. "Pentecost,"vol. 4. Chicago: The Howard-Severance Company, 1915.

Lewis, C. S. *The Screwtape Letters.* New York: Simon & Schuster, 1996.

Metford, J. C. J. *The Christian Year.* New York: Crossroad, 1991.

Pelikan, Jaroslav, *Acts.* Grand Rapids: Brazos, 2005.

Sanders, Fred. *The Deep Things of God: How the Trinity Changes Everything.* Wheaton, Illinois: Crossway, 2010.

Strobel, Lee and Gary Poole. *Experiencing the Passion of Jesus: A Discussion Guide on History's Most Important Event.* Grand Rapids: Zondervan, 2004.

Talley, Thomas J. *Origins of the Liturgical Year.* Liturgical Press, 1986.

Tertullian, *On Baptism,* public domain.

Tickle, Phyllis. *The Divine Hours: Pocket Edition.* Oxford: Oxford University Press, 2007.

Trapp, Maria Augusta. *Around the Year with the Trapp Family.* New York: Pantheon Books Inc. 1955.

Westrheim, Margo. *Celebrate: A look at Calendars and the Ways We Celebrate.* Oxford: Oneworld Publications, 1999.

Winner, Lauren F. *A Cheerful and Comfortable Faith.* New Haven: Yale University Press, 2010.

Winner, Lauren F, "20+C+M+B+06: An Epiphany," *Boundless Webzine,* January 6, 2012, http://www.boundless.org/2005/articles/a0001191.cfm.

Wong, Curtis M, "Epiphany, or Three Kings Day Celebrations Around the World," HuffingtonPost.com, January 6, 2011, http://www.huffingtonpost.com/2011/01/06/epiphany-three-kings-day-photos_n_805245.html#s219869&title=Cyprus_.

Appendix I: Suggestions for Further Reading

In addition to the works our authors mentioned and/or cited throughout this book, we recommend the following books as being helpful for further study of the church year:

Bradshaw, Paul F. and Maxwell E. Johnson. *The Origin of Feasts, Fasts and Seasons in Early Christianity*. London: SPCK, 2011.

Connell, Martin. *Eternity Today, On the Liturgical Year, Vol 2*. New York: Continuum. 2006.

D'Avila-Latourrette, Brother Victor-Antoine. *Twelve Months of Monastery Soups*. New York: Broadway Books, 1998.

Gould, Meredith. *The Catholic Home: Celebrations and Traditions for Holidays, Feast Days, and Every Day*. New York: Image, 2006.

Guite, Malcolm. *Sounding the Seasons: Poetry for the Christian Year*. Norwich: Canterbury Press. 2012.

Hockman-Wet, Cathleen and Mary Beth Lind. *Simply in Season, Expanded Edition*. Scottman, PA: Herald Press, 2009.

Ireton, Kimberlee Conway. *The Circle of Seasons: Meeting God in the Church Year*. Downers Grove, IL: IVP, 2008.

Keble, John. *The Christian Year. Thoughts in verse for the Sundays and Holydays throughout the year*. James Parker and Co.: Oxford and London. 94th edition. 1866.

Rees, Christina. *Feast + Fast: Food for Lent and Easter*. London: Darton, Longman and Todd Ltd., 2011.

Sayers, Dorothy L. *The Man Born to Be King. A Play Cycle on the Life of our Lord and Saviour Jesus Christ*. London: Victor Gollancz Ltd., 1946.

Vitz, Evelyn Birge. *A Continual Feast: A Cookbook to Celebrate the Joys of Family and Faith Throughout the Christian Year.* San Francisco: Ignatius Press, 1991.

Webber, Robert. *Ancient-Future Time: Forming Spirituality through the Christian Year.* Baker, 2004.

Zimmerman, Martha. *Celebrating the Christian Year: Building Family Traditions Around All the Major Christian Holidays.* Bethany House, 1994.

Appendix II: On Celebrating Saints' Days

By Jessica Snell

"Be imitators of me, as I am of Christ."

For someone new to the idea of the church year, the observance of saints' days can be the most strange and unfamiliar part of the whole Christian liturgical tradition. It is easy to associate the celebration of saints' days in the Protestant tradition with the celebration of saints' days in other traditions, and to conclude that avoiding the practice altogether is the safest way to avoid certain theological errors.

But that would be a little like throwing away old family photographs and mementos in an effort to distance oneself from the practice of ancestor worship. The two may be sometimes connected in practice, but they aren't connected by necessity. The observance of saints' days does not have to be a stumbling block. Instead, it can be an encouragement. It can be a reminder, in the middle of our busy and confusing lives, that the Lord Jesus is the same yesterday, today, and forever: He has always guided His people, and He will guide them still.

What is a Saint's Day?

Let us start with what a saint's day is: it is the anniversary of the death of a Christian of renown. Note: it is the anniversary of his death, not of his birth. And that is because, for Christians, the day of death marks the true day of birth – birth into the presence of the Lord. On the day of their death, Christians are born into their new life: born into the presence of the living God, their hope and their Savior.

161

Like most of the feasts and fasts in the western church, most saint's days in our calendar were put in place by the Roman Catholic Church. (There is also an Eastern calendar of saints, established by the Eastern Orthodox Church.) Many mainline Protestant denominations kept these calendars when they separated from Rome, and still use them today.

Why Remember the Saints?

As a person who was raised as a (mostly) non-denominational Christian, and who is now in a liturgical Protestant tradition, the idea of observing saints' days is still somewhat new to me. But what helps me understand this tradition is remembering St. Paul's injunction to "be imitators of me, as I am of Christ." In recognizing the saints, the church is saying, "Look at these people because they did a good job imitating Christ."

As many have noted, it's sometimes hard to answer the question "what would Jesus do?" for the simple reason that you don't happen to be a first-century Jewish male in your thirties – letting alone the fact that you aren't the Messiah! When we look at the saints, we are looking at a wide variety of people who have imitated Christ: priests, missionaries, businessmen, children, fathers, mothers, monks, nuns, even kings and queens! Some of them may be in circumstances a little bit like your own, and their examples can be helpful when you are trying to live your life to the glory of God. And even those saints who are very different than you can give you a better idea of what following and imitating Christ looks like.

Now, you still imitate Christ primarily; the saints can't replace Him in any way, shape, or form. But they're like older brothers and sisters who've been living with your parents' rules longer than you have, and who can show you the ropes. You can look at them, and be encouraged, because they have proven that it's possible to follow Christ in every era, in every country, in every situation, no matter your age, race, or gender.

The Church Triumphant and the Church Militant

The other great benefit of observing the saints' days is the way it can change our perspective on our own fellow church members: the saints who are alive with us today.

Just as we can look to the lives of Christians of the past for examples and for encouragement, we can look around our own local churches. We can look around and see what each person does best, and imitate those virtues in each other. One is good at evangelism, one at ministering to children, another at faithfully cleaning up the sanctuary each week . . . this is the joy of the church: that we many are one body, that everywhere we turn our eyes we can see the Lord's work in redeeming us and in making us more like Him.

Just as we look to those in the past who were really good at following Christ, we can look to those in the present.

And the practice of looking to the saints in the past can help us to see God's work in His people in the present. If you study the lives of the saints of the past, you will see that those glorious, holy men and women were also – as clearly recorded in the histories! – grumpy sinners: sometimes unchaste, sometimes unkind, and sometimes unlovable.

Just like the folks next to us in the pews. Just like ourselves.

And yet, they followed God. They repented, they obeyed, and God used them. If God can use them, He can use us. If they were well loved by the church, the person next to us can be well loved too.

And God will give us the grace to do so.

A Few Resources

For children:
"I Sing a Song of the Saints of God," by Lesbia Scott. This traditional hymn, with its jaunty tune, is the perfect way to introduce children to the idea of saints, and its cheerful words encourage them that they can also follow the Lord, bravely and faithfully, like the saints.

For more serious reading:
"To All Angels and Saints," by George Herbert. This poem is perhaps the best defense and explanation of the traditional Protestant view of the saints ever penned. Herbert acknowledges both his love for God's people of the past and the reason why he cannot pray to them. Beautiful and masterful.
Christ in His Saints, by Fr. Patrick Henry Reardon. An Eastern Orthodox perspective on the saints of the Bible, Fr. Reardon beautifully explains how to look for the Lord's presence and work in the people of scripture.

Scripture Index

Our Writers

JESSICA SNELL is a graduate of Biola University and the Torrey Honors Institute. She is the altar guild directress at her local Anglican parish. She lives with her husband and four children in southern California. Her work has appeared in Touchstone: a Journal of Mere Christianity and she blogs about books, family, and faith at churchyear.blogspot.com.

MICHELLE ALLEN BYCHEK is a wife and mother with a special love for liturgical traditions in the church and home. She works as a speech-language pathologist and lives with her husband and daughter in the central California mountains.

ANN DOMINGUEZ is a writer, doctor, and homeschooling mother of four. Her writing has been published in the Archives of InterVarsity Christian Fellowship, Medical Economics, and JAMA.

ANNA MOSELEY GISSING researches, writes, and speaks about the intersection of faith, family, and contemporary culture. She is a graduate student, a wife, and a mother of young children.

CATE MACDONALD is the Director of The Academy at Houston Baptist University and oversees Staff and Student Care for Wheatstone Ministries. She is interested in sanctification, vocation, the theology of the family, hospitality (both emotional and physical), and educational theory. A Biola University graduate and Member of the Torrey Honors Institute, she has a B.A. in English Literature and an M.A. in Spiritual Formation and Soul Care.

LINDSAY MARSHALL is a high school history teacher, lifelong student, intermittent writer, and avid horseback rider. You can find her thoughts on politics, history, film, and whatever else catches her attention at Wheatstone Academy's The Examined Life (http://wheatstoneministries.com/tel/) or thenarrowgait.com.

JENNIFER SNELL is a clergy spouse in the Anglican Diocese of Fort Worth, Texas. A graduate of Biola University and the Torrey Honors Institute, she is now the homemaker and caregiver for her family of five.

KRISTEN STEWART is a writer and teacher who lives in Nashville, Tennessee with her husband Michael and their daughters, Kate and Lexi.

RACHEL TELANDER's passion for writing is exceeded only by her passion for her faith. She is an active member of her parish, the Anglican church of St. John the Evangelist, and Advent has always been her favorite season of the church year.

About Doulos Resources

Our goal is to provide resources to support the church and kingdom, and to build up and encourage the pastors and leaders within the church. Our resources follow the model of Ephesians 4:12—"to prepare God's people for works of service, so that the body of Christ may be built up." We produce books, curricula, and other media resources; conduct research to advance our goals; and offer advice, counsel, and consultation. We are Reformed and Presbyterian, but not exclusively so; while we do not lay aside our theological convictions, we believe our resources may be useful across a broader theological and ecclesiastical spectrum.

Our goal with *Let Us Keep The Feast*, as with all of our resources, is to offer well-edited, high-quality, and useful materials at an affordable price that makes our resources accessible to congregations and members of the church.

If you are interested in ordering additional copies of *Let Us Keep The Feast*, or to order other materials that Doulos Resources offers, please visit our website: www. doulosresources.org. If you are ordering in quantity for a church or other ministry, contact us to inquire about a discount for quantity orders.

Doulos Resources Contact Information:

U.S. Mail: PO Box 69485, Oro Valley, AZ 85737 USA
Telephone: (901) 201-4612
Internet:
website: www.doulosresources.org
e-mail: info@doulosresources.org

At Doulos Resources, we've found that we often appreciate owning both print and digital editions of the books we read; perhaps you have found this as well.

In our gratitude to you for purchasing a print version of this book, we are pleased to offer you free copies of the digital editions of *Let Us Keep The Feast*. To obtain one or more of these, simply visit our eStore (estore.doulosresources.org) and enter the following discount code during checkout:

LUKTFDigitalDiscount

If you purchased a digital edition, you may use the same discount code to receive a discount deducting the full price of your digital edition off of the purchase price for a print edition.

Likewise, if you purchased the print edition through Amazon.com, you will find that you may obtain the Kindle edition for free through the Kindle Matchbook program.

Thank you for your support!

CPSIA information can be obtained
at www.ICGtesting.com
Printed in the USA
LVHW080420181118
597546LV00005B/111/P